WHEN BLACK WOMEN SPEAK, THE UNIVERSE LISTENS

WHEN BLACK WOMEN SPEAK, THE UNIVERSE LISTENS

a glimpse into our personal power and rightful place in the universe

The world is awaiting your
masterpiece!

Arvat McClaine

Arvat McClaine Ph.D.

ISBN: 1547095547
ISBN 13: 9781547095544

To Harry who makes me feel like the shining star in our unending fairy tale

CONTENTS

CHAPTER 1

THE FEEL OF COTTON

*As long as we are not ourselves, we will
try to be what other people are.*

—*Malidoma Patrice Some'*

O n this surprisingly warm day in January, I was in a trance as I drove the familiar route to my newly built dream home. The hour and a half drive takes me out of the city and into miles and miles of vast, open country land. I pass pastures where cattle graze so lazily and freely. I pass horse ranches and I wonder if the horses ever get tired of standing around doing nothing. I pass huge pig farms and I am always surprised that there is no stench to indicate that they are there. I never fail to see a big beautiful dear on the side of the road who has been introduced to the brute power of an automobile and who has now become the main guest at the table of a dozen shiny black birds that I would be tempted to call crows except their enormity of size makes me think otherwise. On this country drive, I see the straightest, tallest rows of pine trees, and, even though they have naturally grown like that, it is hard to believe that they weren't purposely placed in those exact places to show off their majestic presence.

With no buildings around to block it, the sky is more noticeable here too. The clouds always ensure that no two trips down this country road present the same view. Sometimes they are well-formed, thick white clouds that leave the surrounding sky a blue so deep that it makes you want to meld with it. Sometimes the haze of the clouds is so thin that you barely even notice that they are there, but those are the days when the sky is a soft, powder blue. And, sometimes the message from the sky says, "Take shelter soon!" The dark and even darker grays of the sky predict the torrential rainstorm that is about to nourish the planet around you.

But, the main thing that I notice on my drives on this country route is the land! It is exquisite, expansive, and ever-changing. Depending on the season, you might see rows and rows of green (and later brown) stalks of corn or soy beans or cotton.

Cotton. It is amazing to see the cotton plant. It seems really strange that the fluffy white stuff that so many of our favorite clothes are made from is actually grown from a seed that is planted in the dirt rather than made in a factory by man. I remember the first time that I saw the cotton plants on this road. Mesmerized, I stopped my car on the side of the road because I had to put my hands on this white, puffy substance. And, then I had to have a piece of it for myself.

⇒⇥ ⇤⇐

My husband, Harry, and I named our dream home Uhuru Bluff. The name seems to resonate with all of our family and friends, but few have any idea of why we chose that name. A couple of months earlier, Harry and I had hiked Mount Kilimanjaro in Tanzania, the highest mountain in Africa. Making that trek, almost 20,000 feet into the sky, walking between 8-14 hours each day, took us through a variety of terrains and climate changes. On our first day of the climb up the mountain, we were quite toasty in our short sleeves and thin hiking pants. The air was thick and humid and filled with the smells of the lush vegetation and abundant exotic animals. By the fourth day of the hike, I had on two pairs of thermals, a pair of running tights, a pair of sweat pants and a pair of windproof pants on my bottom half. On the top, I had all of those same layers plus two coats. There was no vegetation anywhere to break the winds that were whipping so strongly that Natori, my Tanzanian guide, literally had to hold me to weight me down to keep me from being blown off our course. The air this high up is so thin and weak with oxygen that I could only take 1 or 2 steps at a time before needing to stop to catch my breath.

The top of this mountain is called the Uhuru Peak. Uhuru is a Tanzanian word for "freedom". But to us, Uhuru also meant facing an obstacle head-on, taking it one step at a time, going as far as you can go, and enjoying the process along the way.

Our dream home, Uhuru Bluff, is located in Smithfield, Isle of Wight County, Virginia. It is within walking distance to the historic Fort Huger which is the site of an abandoned American Civil War fort. This was a strategic Confederate Army fort that is on a bluff that overlooks the James River, built to keep the Union Army from advancing towards Richmond, the then capital of the Confederacy. The fort was built by enslaved and free Black men.

Like our neighbor, Fort Huger, our home is also located on a bluff. But that is not the only reason we decided to call our home Uhuru Bluff. Bluff has another meaning too. When someone bluffs, they are pretending or trying to lead you to believe something that is not true. While we really have no way of knowing, Harry and I believe that many of those Black men, enslaved and free, were only bluffing (both to themselves and others) while lending their help to the Confederate Army. Some of them may have been invested in protecting their short-term interests, but in the long-run, it is not likely that they wanted things to remain as they were during that bleak time in American history.

Our little slice of heaven in Smithfield, Virginia—Uhuru Bluff—at once, conjures up images of our tumultuous past and of overcoming obstacles on our trek to the type of freedom that everyone craves and deserves.

⊯ ⊱

By now, the country road is so familiar to me, that it was easy for me to slip into a trance on that mild January day as I rode past all the facets of nature that typically awe me. But, I was suddenly jarred out of autopilot mode, and I looked out of the right side of my window. The crops that fill the fields at other times of the year were all gone. But because we had been having an abnormally warm winter season, grass was beginning to grow in fields that should have been dormant. The grass was that shade of green that you only associate with spring and it blanketed the land as far as the eye could see. It was beautiful.

And, though, I do not honestly know who owns any of that land, all I could think was the same thought that I often think when making this long country drive: "This is the land where my ancestors shed their blood, sweat, and tears picking that thorny cotton in the heat of the sun." Visions flood my mind of the on-going labor of the men, women, and children who look like me who had no other choices but to endure or to die. I see the keloid scars on the backs and arms of my grandfathers and I hear the muffled screams of violation from my grandmothers from generations past. And I am angry.

And the thoughts through my mind flow so quickly like a movie on fast-forward through the few hundred years of slavery, through the lynchings and the Jim Crow Era, through the Civil Rights Movement, through the crack epidemic, through jails over-represented by faces like mine, through over-crowded and underfunded schools, through low-paying jobs and hungry children, through the mothers crying due to their sons being killed by their own peers or by the men in blue who are sworn to protect us and much, much more.

And, I think of how America is known as the land of opportunity. Everyone has a chance to make it here. We have unalienable rights.

And, if you don't make it here, then it must be your own fault.

But, the playing field is not even. Black hands worked that land. But the generations that followed did not *physically* benefit from that labor. There was no plot of land, no money in a bank account to pass on to the next generation.

Typically, my next thought would have been along the lines of, "That's why we have to work twice as hard to arrive at the finish line. We need to buckle down and just do what we have to do."

But on this mild January day, I had a different thought. "There has got to be another way!" I thought. "Why are we playing a game where we keep ending up on the losing team? Why can't we play a different game?"

CHAPTER 2
THIS AND THAT

*If one is lucky, a solitary fantasy can
totally transform one million realities.*

—*Maya Angelou*

How can a man spend 27 years in prison and emerge as the face of peace that transforms hate in a highly racialized country? How can a man have a dream in 1963 that still lives on today in the hearts of millions? How can a woman secure her own freedom from enslavement and then make 19 return trips to bring 300 other people to freedom?

President Nelson Mandela, Dr. Martin Luther King, Jr., and Harriet Tubman were well aware of the dire straits that they and the world that they lived in faced. The world that their eyes could see was a bleak place. Around them every day was a blatant disregard for human life that was sustained by a system of unjust laws and an ideology that some people—white people—were more deserving than others and that some people—Black people—were of an inferior race.

Despite the reality that they faced, they all had something in common. They all had a dream. Whether from a cramped prison cell or from the segregated south or from the confines of slavery, they all were able to transcend their current-day reality and exchange it for a dream that suited them (and the world) better. Each of their personal dreams was wide enough to embrace all of humanity and was able to infuse people with an energy that was more powerful than hate, fear, and even the indifference associated with maintaining the status quo.

Throughout my life, I have pondered what it must take for someone to go against all of the odds and to make a break for freedom when captivity is all that you know. How did Harriet (I hope she wouldn't mind me calling her by her first name, but I have carried her with me all of my life, so I feel like we have a personal relationship) know that what was on the other side was worth taking the risks? How do you motivate yourself to attempt that escape when you know they are coming after you with pointed guns and barking dogs and readied whips? How do you make yourself leave when you know you will have to outthink, outwit, and outrun your would-be captors? How do you make yourself go on when you know you are going to be crawling through swampy swamps, sleeping under prickly bushes, traveling through creepy woods in the night, and always on high-alert, possibly jumping at every crackle of the forest around you? And then, when you get to sweet freedom, you go back. You do it all over again—a whopping 19 more times!

I use my imagination to glimpse at her source of inspiration. In my imagination, I see that she has used her imagination to envision a world where all people are free. She sees a world where all people are treated with dignity and respect; a world where you get to love the people that you love; you get to do the things that you want to do; you get to choose the life that you want to have; you get to explore your options, live into your possibilities, and create a life of happiness. Isn't that dream worth the risks?

Our society is very different now. The language of the law has changed. There are few laws left on the books that explicitly state that differential treatment due to race is legal. Men like Former President Barak Obama and Governor Douglass Wilder changed the idea of what is possible for little Black boys. The existence of women, like Former First Lady Michelle Obama and Oprah Winfrey, help to expand the definition of what is achievable for little Black girls.

Yet, much of the same ideology of hate, fear, and discrimination still lurks in our justice system, our political system, our educational system, and our healthcare system. African Americans lag behind their white counterparts on practically every standard of living scale with less access to well-paying jobs, quality housing, and neighborhood grocery stores. Amongst other things, African Americans are faced with higher interest rates, higher crime rates, and a higher incidence of single-parent homes.

I could go on about our current-day struggles. The story has been repeatedly told. We all know the story by heart. It is a part of our conscious and unconscious psyche. We believe it to be true.

The funny thing about beliefs is that the more people that hold a belief, the stronger the belief becomes. Due to centuries of mistreatment on this continent, we *really* believe in our struggle, in our lack, and in our dismal circumstances. Like Mandela, King and Tubman, we have to consider whether we want the belief that we currently have to be our continued reality. Or do we want to dream a new dream, a different dream, one potent enough to change the world?

Well, if you are like me, you might be thinking, "I am struggling to keep myself and my family straight. How can I change the world?" What I have come to realize is that by living your best life and by making your dreams come true, you actually are doing that—you are changing the world. Think of how that little, enslaved woman (who had fainting spells) in Dorchester County, Maryland followed in the direction of her dreams and helped 300 individuals to freedom but her legacy inspires many generations beyond. By the same token, everyone who witnesses you dreaming your own unique dream and witnesses you creating the life that you want will be affected by your actions. They will believe it is possible for them to do the same. Your actions today can create a rippling effect that lasts all of eternity.

Just think, as you choose what you want from the delicious, hearty buffet that we call life, you are simultaneously inviting others to share in this dessert with you. Life is not "either/or"; it is "both/and". You really can "have your cake and eat it too."

CHAPTER 3

TOO SMART FOR YOUR OWN GOOD

You are far too smart to be the only thing standing in your way.

—*Jennifer J. Freeman*

"Kick it into gear!" I heard someone say.

"Run faster!" another voice shouted at me.

"You can do it! Don't let them catch you!" screamed yet another voice in a crowd of many.

"What the heck are they talking about?" I thought. "I am in my highest gear! I can't go any faster!"

But I didn't know how close they were. I didn't know if they would overtake me in the very next second or not. So,

I gave it everything that I had left in me. If I wasn't going to win, it was not going to be because I didn't try.

Many years earlier, in my days at The Ohio State University, I had a friend who used to tell me that I was too smart for my own good. She usually made this statement right after I had successfully defended my position and left everyone with nothing else to say. If I had any time to feel proud of myself for my verbal gymnastics and quick ability to logically break down the subject and reconstruct it in such a way as to make everyone see my point, it was truly short-lived. My friend would look at me and shake her head ever so slightly and I could hear the subtle tone of admonishment in her voice as she would say, "You are too smart for your own good."

I didn't know what she meant when she said it, but I knew that I needed to check myself. Even after we had gone our separate ways, whenever I had that verbal victory, rather than take a moment to feel proud of what I had just done, I would hear her voice in my head, "You are too smart for your own good." And, I felt a feeling that is a close relative to being ashamed.

Her words always caused me to review the scorecard word for word, blow by blow. But I could never identify the error.

Then I met David. In David, I had met my match. Debating with him was like a day at the Olympics. We battled like the top competitors in gymnastics, swimming, and track and field all at once. We were both crafty in the way we were able to swerve in and out of holes that the other had temporarily boxed us into. We both knew how to make our words flow as smoothly as the synchronized swimmers. And we both were as quick on our feet as Usain Bolt. Our rounds would last for hours. We often would call a "draw" due to sheer exhaustion. Occasionally, one or the other of us would emerge victoriously. And in those moments, we both admired the other for a job well-done.

David eventually married a beautiful woman who had no skills nor desires to enter into the Olympic games. She knew what she knew, she thought what she thought, and she believed what she believed. That was it. There was no dissertation attached to why she thought or felt a certain way. No, she couldn't explain how she came to that position. No, she couldn't prove the things that she just knew in her heart. And, no, she didn't know why whatever David was saying didn't make any sense despite his well-developed arguments that seemed to suggest that he was the authority on the subject.

However, oftentimes, I had drawn the same conclusions as she had. And, the strategies that I would employ to prove or defend my point of view would dance effortlessly across my mind. I would have been able to cause him to pause to consider what I was saying rather than toss her ideas away as if she had never said anything.

Watching their dynamic was the light that I needed to understand that ever-present voice in my head, "You are too smart for your own good." Mind you, I was having the exact same dynamic play out in my own home. Harry also felt what he felt and he knew what he knew. But, it was easy for me to dismiss whatever he was saying because he couldn't "prove it to me" or "explain it to me like I'm an 8-year-old." Unable to *logically* explain his position to me, he would acquiesce to whatever *I* thought to be the thing that made the most sense. Blind to the dynamic, I was shocked when I overheard a conversation between my brother and him:

"Whew!" my brother said. "She knows how to use those words."

"I know," Harry said. "Sometimes I can be telling her the truth about something that happened and she will ask me so many questions that I get confused. By the time she is done, *I believe* I was lying!"

I finally got it! I really was too smart for my own good!

Although I wasn't abusive in my language or delivery, I was actually verbally abusing people who happened to be less adept at using the English language, less linear in their thinking, possibly less well-read, and not quite as quick on their feet as I was. I was invalidating their other ways of knowing the world around them. I was making them wrong. And I was not valuing their contributions. Simply put, I could not hear them.

Only being able to hear your own voice or other voices just like yours closes you off to an entire world of possibilities.

In addition, I eventually came to realize that I could rationalize anything. I can always make myself "right" and I can always make someone else "wrong". Simply put, I could fool myself. (And, even more simply put, I was a fool!)

⚒ ⚒

I had been training for this moment for 2 solid months. I had received a phone call telling me that I had been randomly selected to be the contestant who would have an opportunity to run in a well-known race against the elite runners for a cash prize. The caller convinced me to say, "Yes" to this exciting yet scary prospect by explaining that I would get a fair head start. The event organizers would calculate how much of a head start I would get by plugging my finishing time from the previous year into a formula to determine how far I should be able to run in the amount of time that they estimated the actual winner of the race to finish the event. I was told they would then make it a little more challenging than the calculated distance so that I would have to work for it.

Since I am not afraid of hard work, I agreed to take the challenge. I hired a running coach and round and round I ran on the track at my top speeds. I began doing Bikram Yoga almost daily and getting sports massages weekly in order to keep my body injury-free. I did leg-strengthening exercises, foam rolled my legs, reduced other forms of exercise, and invested in a lighter pair of running shoes. I was serious.

After being featured in the newspaper and on television a few times, everywhere I went, people were rooting for me. I was confident that I was doing everything that I could be doing, so I thought I would be victorious on race day...until I got the phone call from the event organizers telling me how much of a head start I was actually being given.

"In previous years, the contestant usually finishes about a block ahead of the elites. This year, we tweaked our formula because we want it to be a real battle to the finish to make the crowd go wild," I was told.

"No, please don't do that to me," I pleaded.

"You will be fine. So what if you don't win?" he said. "It's just for fun."

Fun for whom? I wondered.

I reported the head start information to my running coach, Jason, in hope that he would say, "Yes, Arvat, you can still win if you put your mind to it." But he, too, was disturbed by the numbers. He wrote a letter to the event organizers that very clearly proved to them why, with the limited head start that they were giving me, that I had no chance of winning. Furthermore, there would be no battle to the finish. According to his calculations, the winner would pass me when I was still 3 blocks away from the finish line. There would be no crowds going wild.

I was defeated before I ever toed the line. It was not possible for me to win this race that I had trained so hard for. I was going to let everyone down.

"There is just no way I can win now. I have been training as hard as I can. I can't believe they waited until just two weeks before the race to tell me this," I said to my mom, moping because all of my spunk had been sapped.

"That's not true," she said. "Remember how you bent time driving from Ohio? Tell yourself you are going to do that again. Go through a time-warp."

Before she even finished her sentence, I had that "eureka" moment!

"Yes, yes!" I said. "I am going to create a miracle!"

Sometimes miracles happen in life, but it is easy for us to brush them off as coincidences. But my life has been sprinkled with sweet little surprises that would suggest that a power greater than me had pulled some strings to make sure that all was ok in my world; and since the age of 12, I was clear that bonafide Moses-era types of miracles really do happen.

"Why" I had asked so many times, "did I have to come here? Why was I ever born? Did God really create me just to allow me to suffer?"

In my mind, for many years, I could see this string. The string was unraveled at the end and exposed this ever so thin thread. I always felt that I was hanging on to this tiny thread from this string that connected me to life. And, I always felt that if I just let this thread snap, then, boom! I would be dead.

It was both a comfort and unsettling to me to know that I had the power to decide when I would let that thread snap. It comforted me to know that when I was just so fed up and I couldn't take it anymore, I could snap the thread and it would be all over with. I could make the pain stop.

But it unsettled me to know that it was up to me to decide when to snap the thread. What if I just thought that I couldn't take it anymore when really, I could? What if I snapped the thread too early? Or, what if I never had the courage to snap the thread and I never made the pain stop? That had really been an ongoing theme in my life—to have the power but not the courage. Then what good are you?

On a warm day when I was 12, I was supposed to be walking to 7-11 to pick up a snack for the school party. But, I really did not have any intention of going to 7-11 because I was not going to the school party. I had decided that I had had enough. I just could not go on any longer. Life had become simply unbearable.

There was no light in my days. I had been sad for as long as I could remember. Maybe worse than sad. No matter how much I smiled, no matter how much I laughed, barely beneath the surface was nothing but darkness, doom, dread. I hated myself. I hated my life. And, maybe, just maybe, I was beginning to hate God too.

And it seemed that my life was stuck on sorrow. Each moment felt like hours and days felt like months. Will I ever get to the good part? Is there a good part?

Almost without thinking about it, I knew what I was going to do. I was going to wait. I waited for the huge city bus that goes barreling through my neighborhood. When it came, I waited until I was certain that it would be impossible for it to stop, and I walked right out in front of it. BAM! SMASH! And then floating away to a world of no pain is what I thought was going to happen.

I looked into the bus driver's eyes and I saw a look on his face that I don't think I had ever witnessed before or since. The BAM! was taking a long time to happen. And then I knew why the bus driver had that look on his face. The BAM! never happened. The bus stopped on a dime. There was no screeching, no swerving. Just a stopped bus. I returned the bus driver's gaze and I probably had the same look on my face as he had. We had both just been players in a miracle.

I continued walking across the street as if nothing had happened. I decided that I had better go get that snack from 7-11 after all. I was going to be around for a while.

As I walked, I pondered what did this all mean? A miracle? For me? A life-saving miracle? I chose to believe that I was saved because God wanted me to live. I chose to believe that my birth was purposeful and that I was simply being prepared to do something great. I would need the strength that I was building in order to successfully accomplish this great mission before me. If God thinks I am up for the task, then so do I. Who am I to believe anything different?

I decided that never again would I consider letting my thread snap or attempt to take my life. No matter how hard, no matter how sad.

⇒+⇐

During my junior year in college, I traveled with a friend to Cleveland, Ohio for Spring break. The week flew by perfectly. By noon on our final Sunday, the car was packed, we had said our goodbyes to family and friends, and we hopped in the car to begin our 8-hour journey back to school in Virginia. We buckled our seat belts and turned the key in the ignition. Nothing happened. The car would not start.

Over the course of that day, my friend's grandfather had a variety of men file through to try their hand at getting the car started. Everything seemed fine with the car except no gas was flowing. Although I kept saying that the problem was in the trunk (because the car was fine until we packed our luggage into the trunk), none of the men could determine what was going on with the car. The car was a brand-new car at a time when fuel injection systems were new on the scene. These men knew how to work on carburetors, but they were clueless about fuel injection systems.

As the hours ticked away, I became very antsy. My college had the policy that if you miss a class the day before or the day after a holiday, that would count as 2 absences. If you had 3 absences, you would automatically fail the class. Well, I had already missed one day, so if I did not make it to school in time for my 8 a.m. class, then I would fail that class. I really needed that car to be fixed by midnight in order to make the 8-hour drive and get to class on time.

Tick tick tick 8 o'clock, 9 o'clock, 10 o'clock—the men continued to ignore me as I told them it was something to do with the trunk. I prayed with everything in me and my heart raced because I *could not* miss my morning class. Tick tick tick 11 o'clock, midnight, 1 o'clock. Now it was too late. There was no way I could make it to my class now. After all of the prayer and the stress of the day, I finally relaxed. There was no hope now. It was a done deal.

Tick tick, finally, a man decided to read the owner's manual. What did he find? There was a fuel pump shut-off switch that would shut down the flow of gas to the car if the car was impacted with force. Where was the switch? In the trunk. We had literally rammed our luggage into the trunk of the car prior to attempting to leave which caused us a 14-hour delay! But at 2 o'clock, we had finally hit the road for our journey back to Virginia.

We managed to get on the road in good spirits. My anxiety about failing my class had settled and I decided to just enjoy the ride. We predicted that this usual 8-hour drive would be closer to 9 or 10 hours because we were certainly doomed to run into the bumper to bumper Washington, D.C. morning rush hour traffic. Nevertheless, we drove happily laughing and chatting as the miles went by.

"Did that sign just say Washington, D.C.?" I said.

"No, you are seeing things," my friend said.

We had only been driving for 2 hours, so seeing a Washington, D.C. sign so soon did not make sense.

"Hey, that sign does say Washington, D.C.," my friend said as we approached yet another sign that indicated that Washington, D.C. was about 80 miles away. Now we were puzzled. We both fell silent.

"How could this have happened?" I said, pulling out the map of the route we were supposed to be taking. "Do you think we took a different route that got us here faster?"

"No, I didn't drive off course," my friend said.

It was 6:45 a.m. when I pulled into my dorm at school. I had time to take a quick nap, a shower, and get to my 8 o'clock class on time.

I don't get to talk to my old friend much anymore, but whenever we do talk, we always say, "Remember that drive when we traveled through time?"

⇥⇤

But those miracles happened to and for me. I didn't make those things happen, did I? At first glance, I thought I was moving into new territory. But then I remembered times when maybe I did create the miracle—like meeting Harry or like acing my chemistry exams when chemistry only presented itself as a foreign language to me.

One day when Harry and I had returned to my old room at my mom's house to collect some things, we came across a story that I had typed and put in its own yellow binder. It was a story I had written as a pre-teen while sitting on the beach years before I had met Harry. The story was about me meeting a boy on a bus who ended up being my new neighbor. His family had just moved in across the street from me. (Harry's family had moved in next door to me.) The boy had 5 siblings (Harry has 5 siblings) and his physical description matched Harry's. The boy in the story and I grew up together, went to college separately, got back together after college, started a psychology practice together (Harry and I started a mental health agency together) and lived happily ever after.

So clear is the memory of the day that I wrote the story that I now say was about Harry. I had been playing in the waters at the beach all day with my brothers and mom. I separated myself out from them and I sat, facing the waters. I breathed deeply and I went to that place where it almost feels like a dream, but you are wide awake. Every detail of the story had to be perfect. I remember coming up with scenarios, and then erasing them in my mind, and replacing them with details that I liked better. When I was done, I repeated the story over and over in my mind so that I would not forget the details. When we returned home from the beach, I rushed to type the story and placed it in the most perfect yellow binder. Why? I had never done such a thing before nor since.

Then there was chemistry. Being naturally gifted in maths and sciences, it baffled me that I was unable to get a grasp on chemistry. I studied at every opportunity to no avail. Before every exam, I barricaded doors, turned off phones, and completely shut out all outside distractions as I thoroughly and repeatedly reviewed my lessons. This ritual of concentrated effort did absolutely nothing to enhance my understanding.

The last thing that I would do before my exams is calm myself. I would pray. I would also think of scientists like George Washington Carver and Mae Jemison.

"Please help me with my exam," I would say. "Help me to use my brain in the way that you use yours. Pour your knowledge into me."

Though I had prepared all that I could, I would enter into the classroom feeling woefully unprepared to take the exam. I go into test-taking mode and the rest of the world fades. It is just me and the exam. That is until the first student completes his exam and leaves the classroom. How can he be done already? I'm not even a third of the way finished. I feel sorry for him because I realize that he must not have known what he was doing so he just wrote anything, or worse, gave up. Soon, though, another and another student turn in their papers. And, finally, with half of the exam left to complete, I am the last one in the classroom still taking the exam. My heart is racing and I feel like I surely am not doing this correctly.

After I turn in my paper, there is no reason to even look over my lessons to try to determine if I did everything right. I didn't understand my lessons. I didn't understand the exam. And I had no idea of what I wrote. So, I wait it out until our papers are returned at our next class session. I sneak peaks at the other students' grades as their papers are returned. The grades don't look too good and there is a general gloom over the classroom.

When the professor hands me my paper, I hesitate to look at it. I am sieged with fear. I fold my paper so that no wandering eyes can see my grade. I got an A—to my knowledge, the only A in the class.

I suppose you can imagine my surprise the first few times this scenario played out, but I took 4 semesters of chemistry and I continued to be equally surprised after each and every exam. But I continued to follow my winning formula to the letter—study as much as I could, pray, and envision the scientific geniuses and ask them for help.

Doing well on an exam may not seem like much of a miracle to you, but I couldn't have understood chemistry any less if it had been written in hieroglyphics.

My life hasn't been short in the miracles department and it seemed like I had the elements I needed. I was armed with the belief that I could create a miracle for myself. My travel from Ohio to Virginia convinced me that it was possible to move through time and space in unexpected and illogical ways. And though I didn't learn much chemistry, chemistry did teach me that I had the ability to tap into other people's knowledge base.

Now, I *believed* that I could win that race—but I wasn't *sure*.

I continued to work as hard as I could to prepare. But I also actively created an arsenal of thoughts that buoyed me and shored up my faith. The presence of a butterfly one beautiful spring day provided me with an important key to put into place. As I walked outdoors, this delicate butterfly came close enough to me that it gave me a quick little tickle all over my body. The butterfly did not physically touch me, yet I felt its fluttering. I realized that I had experienced this before with butterflies and even with buzzing flies and bumble bees. But if these flying insects are not actually touching me, why am I able to feel the ripple of their presence all over my body?

Aha, that tiny winged creature had flown into my field of energy, I thought. And I pictured myself bigger, more expansive than any mirror-image of me might suggest. I saw an energy surrounding me that radiated out in all directions from me into infinity. In my mind's eye, I saw this energy to be similar to an ombre' dress I had seen where the color at the top of the dress was a rich deep purple. As your eye travels down the dress, the deep purple gradually changes to a shade slightly lighter and then lighter still until, at the bottom of the dress, it was a pale lilac so light that it was almost white. Except, I didn't really see color; I saw concentrated energy close to my body. As I radiated outward, my energy field became less and less concentrated. Eventually, it was like the bottom of the dress, so faint that you almost couldn't see it.

At first, I didn't make the connection. It was just a pleasant thought floating around in my head. It was a cool visual to have because I consciously recognized that we are literally interacting with *everyone* at all times. The further away you are from someone, the fainter this interaction becomes, so you don't even notice it. But like the pale, almost white lilac of the dress, the interaction is still there, your presence matters. You make a difference.

Soon enough, though, I was back on the track, running around and around, hitting the paces that Jason, my coach, wanted me to hit, running faster than I ever had before and breathing so hard that I couldn't breathe.

"This is my last lap," I told myself as I used sheer will to push myself to take each next step.

As I zoom past my would-be stopping point to start yet another lap, I think, "I don't care what Jason says, I'm not doing another lap because I am not trying to die out here."

Jason runs diagonally across the field to meet me at each quarter of the track and shouts out my paces to indicate if I need to speed up, slow down, or if I am on target. "Whether I am on pace or not, I am already doing the best I can do," I think to myself. At my next quarterly update, if my pace has dropped, I shift to a higher gear, because, after all, *this* lap really is going to be my last lap!

And, just when I think I have expended my last drop of energy, Jason joins me in the run. He is talking to me, but I don't know what he is saying. I am on the verge of delirium.

"Either you want me to run or you want me to listen to you. I can't do both," I think to myself.

But, as I match my pace to his, I feel like we are slowing down. This lap feels easier than all the rest. My body relaxes just a bit and I can breathe again. I am ok. I am thankful for this reprieve. When he calls out the pace, I am shocked! I am still on target! How could that be? Hadn't we slowed way down?

For a moment, I thought he had been mistaken. But then I realized that I always did run much faster when I ran with people who were faster than me. As a matter of fact, I also run faster and easier when there are crowds cheering and rooting me on.

I thought about the effect of that butterfly in my energy field and the ombre' dress.

I knew that since I was getting a head start in the race, I would be running by myself. I also knew that the crowd support would be thin at the start of the race but that the streets would be crowded with spectators the closer I moved to the finish line. I made a mental note, "If I start getting tired and feel that I can't go on, *lean in*." *Lean in* towards the crowd. *Lean in* towards their energy. Physically and mentally, I needed to lean my body closer to theirs so that I could experience the richest tones of their energy field interacting to the richest tones of my own field. I needed to allow their energy to do for me what I may not have been able to do for myself.

Another key that I put into place was the only lesson I learned from my chemistry classes. I called upon the greats. In my mind, I conjured up images of Florence Griffith-Joyner (Flo-Jo), Jackie Joyner-Kersee, Jesse Owens, and Usain Bolt. I asked them to help me move my body the way that they move(d) their bodies. I asked them to help me activate that part of my brain that would cause me to run fast; that part of my brain that would allow me to endure; and that part of my spirit that would allow me to keep pushing when the average person would give up.

I flooded my mind with images of times when the impossible was made possible—like the bus that stopped on a dime, like the 8-hour trip that was completed in 5 hours, like stories of women who did amazing feats such as rescuing their children by lifting flipped cars in order to pull their children to safety.

Similar to how I created and then replayed over and over the story of Harry and me, I envisioned myself getting across that line first and breaking the winner's tape over and over again. I prayed. I kept getting the impression in my mind and spirit that race day was the day that

I was going to get my wings. (I didn't exactly know what that meant but I felt that it was going to be a turning point for me, a new freedom of sorts.) And I truly *believed* that I was going to create a miracle that day, but I still wasn't *sure*.

⟞⟞ ⟝⟝

I cried my eyes out on race day when I first approached the starting line. Good news, though, it was a windy day and the wind would be at my back. I also got word that the super-fast guy who was expected to win this event had decided to drop out of this event! Awesome—miracles were already taking place for me! Soon, I saw members of my exercise group (SEAL Team PT) there to support me. They, along with Harry and Jason, were so full of cheer and confidence in me that I dried my eyes.

The race began and all I could hear was Jason coaching my steps as he ran on the sidewalk alongside the race course and "Hooyahs" (the SEAL Team PT cheer) from the members of my exercise group who offered excited support on every block. Still, my breathing was labored and I never knew if I could take the next step. I was always worried that I was going to just have to stop and walk. Soon, other members of my exercise group began running alongside me on the sidewalk. Their presence gave me the extra drive. And, I knew if it was humanly possible, I was NOT going to let them down. BUT, that didn't change the fact that I couldn't breathe! "I HAVE to make it! I just HAVE to," I said. So, I pushed on.

When I got to the last statue on the race course, I could feel a ton of people jump on the course and start running behind me! "Just lean in," I thought. "Lean on them. Coast on their energy." Then, BAM! I saw my wings sprout from my back, they were huge, heavenly wings like those of Pegasus. I marveled at those wings as they allowed me to coast for a couple of blocks as if I had taken flight. Thank goodness because I was on the verge of passing out from not being able to breathe!

Reality came back, and I was 400 meters from the finish line. I had no idea how close the lead runners were to me. I could hear everyone screaming and telling me to kick it into gear!

"Four hundred meters, I got this; I have done this many times before," I thought. But those 400 meters seemed to span a mile.

"Please just keep running. Don't stop now. You MUST keep going," I could hear my own voice saying in my head.

Finally, the winner's tape. I did it! WE DID IT!!

It is so easy for me to get in my head, tune everything and everybody else out and just rely on my inner strength, but my inner strength wasn't enough to get me through this, so I relied on everyone else to pull me through. Every word of encouragement, every cheer, every poster, every positive thought sent my way pooled together to create a miracle for me. But I had to be open to receive the flow of energy that was there present for me. This experience helped me to spread my wings that day, and now I know I can fly!

Having had this experience, you would think that I now regularly rely on the energy that surrounds me and that I create many mini-miracles every day in my life. But, no, sometimes I am still too smart for my own good. It has been incredibly easy for me to revert back to my old ways of doing things. When I am faced with big challenges in life, I can almost immediately remember to seek out help from that flow of energy that is ever-present around me. I remember to pray and to visualize and to ask the experts for help. I remember to set my sights on creating a miracle. But for everyday sorts of things, I rely on my own intellect, my own thoughts, and my own strengths. I figure out how to get things done in my life and it usually all works for the good.

But sometimes I run into a snag. Maybe I am having a disagreement with a friend who I find to be totally unreasonable. Maybe I can't get my washer and dryer delivered because the folks at the appliance store are totally incompetent. Maybe my home repair job is taking way too long because, you know, you can never rely on construction workers. Maybe I can't take the first step towards something I really want to do because, umm, now is not the time (translation, I'm afraid).

After venting and complaining to everyone who will listen, I remember.

I remember that ombre' dress and my energy field that ripples its way clear to infinity. I remember that I am interacting with everyone, simultaneously, no matter how faintly my field appears. I remember that my presence matters. What I do matters. What I think matters. So, I change what I am thinking. I shift my thoughts and feelings from frustration, low expectations, anger, and fear to a feeling of love towards whomever or whatever situation I was dealing with. And magically, miraculously, the situation resolves itself.

Rather than rely on the confines of my limited view and knowledge of the world and continue to butt my head against the wall, I am learning to be open to the field of energy that is available to me more frequently. Rather than allow myself to slip into a state of struggle, I am choosing more often to recognize that I don't have to know everything because I am able to interact with a field that goes on to infinity. As I learn to give up the need to flex my own muscle and to force my own agenda, I realize that I am gaining everything. If I see my old friend, I will tell her that I finally understand the many levels of her statement, "You are too smart for your own good."

CHAPTER 4
OBEY YOUR MAMA

If there is no struggle, there is no progress.

—*Frederick Douglass*

I was at my mom's house one day and she got a call from a friend. I overheard my mom say, "I'm trying to hang in there. Yes, taking one day at a time. Trying to make ends meet."

Upon hearing this, I initially became alarmed. What was she saying? What was she in need of? I thought that I had put everything in place to ensure that she had everything that she needed. And, I knew I had told her on several occasions that if she needed or wanted anything, just let me know.

As soon as she hung up the phone, I said, "Mama, what things do you need?"

"Nothing," she said.

"Well, what things do you want?"

"Nothing, I have everything I need and want," she said but now searching my face trying to figure out what I was getting at.

"I just heard you tell Angie that you are 'trying to hang in there' and are 'trying to make ends meet.'"

"Oh, that's just something you say," she said.

Really? I had heard those expressions many times, but it had never occurred to me that people didn't necessarily mean what they were saying. Why would you make an undesirable claim about yourself? Why would you paint a false image of struggle? I decided to keep my ears open for this kind of banter.

To my surprise, the mouth that I heard it come out of was my own!

"I can't win for losing," I heard my mouth say.

Huh? Where did that come from? I can honestly say that I do not believe those words about myself as a general rule. I am typically happy with the way things turn out for me. But in the moment that I said it, I sure believed it.

Why did those words roll so easily off my tongue? As I thought about it, the memories came flooding back. That was a favorite saying of both my mom and my dad. A chuckle always followed the expression which was said with a frustrated humor.

I remembered other expressions that they said, too, like, "If it wasn't for bad luck, I would have no luck at all" or "With my luck_____ (fill in with a negative consequence)" or "It's no need in me entering the contest 'cuz

I never win anything" or "It's no need in me even looking 'cuz I can never find a good parking space".

And, yes, I have believed and repeated those very words over and over in my life. At first glance, these little sayings may seem harmless, but when we begin to understand the power of our thoughts and our beliefs, we begin to see that it can be our very words that hold us from all that we want in life. A constant repetition of these types of sayings have the potential to create a self-image that would suggest that this world is conspiring against you. These sayings imply that you have to accept whatever the world throws at you—and this world is just throwing shade or hard times your way.

I realize another thing too. We admire the act of struggle. I can't tell you the number of conversations I have heard (and participated in) over the years where folks are comparing their struggles and number of obstacles they have had to overcome. If mine was hard, then yours was harder. If yours was hot, then mine was hotter. If I was sick, then you were sicker. It's kind of funny when you really think about it. Why do we *want* to be the one with the shortest end of the stick?

In our society, we do see struggle as a noble thing. The act of struggle is what makes you strong. You appreciate and value what you have worked hard to earn. Being able to endure this tough situation prepares you for the next. Being a victor in this situation infuses you with another level of self-esteem and confidence.

Those who struggle and win become our heroes and heroines. We love to hear the stories of women like Oprah Winfrey and Maya Angelou who overcame sexual and emotional abuse. And my personal favorite is Harriet Tubman who masterfully exchanged bondage for freedom. These women were polished by the fire, and then they became some of our brightest examples of not only Black women but of human beings. The harder the struggle, the sweeter the reward.

Years ago, I co-founded an African-centered school. In many ways, it was a magical little place. In addition to having the opportunity to excite young minds, the school brought people from all walks of life into my awareness. The school was a magnet for all things African, many of which simply blew my mind! Yet, there was that element— the need to struggle. Every conference that I attended, big or small, the word *struggle* was highlighted.

I always understood that the people who proudly proclaimed, "The struggle continues" or "We will continue this struggle," had the intention of motivating us to continue to take action in the direction of our true freedom while simultaneously reminding us of the trials and bravery of those who walked the road before us. Still, those words never quite sat right with me. I could never quite understand why someone would project struggle into our future. A future of struggle is not motivating to me. It saps my energy. It makes me feel beat-down before I even get started. When you are *always* on the losing team, when you feel there is no chance of winning no matter what you do, you lose some of your drive and competitive edge.

I am so much more inspired by a message of, "Yes we can!" than a message of, "They are not going to let you get ahead. They keep beating you down." I would rather hear about a future of liberty and happiness and of the possibilities. That is what drives me to action and makes me show up with my game face on.

I hear this message of struggle and lack repeated so frequently in our daily conversations, in our churches, on our television screens, "We are all struggling—struggling with our finances, struggling with our health, struggling with our relationships." And I remember when, for many years of my life, that was true for me; I was always struggling with something. I was lucky if I had a day or two between the time one struggle presented itself until the next struggle showed its spiteful head.

But these days, the equation has been flipped. I spend my life in a state of joy that is occasionally interrupted by a few days of struggle. And, sometimes I feel weird that I am no longer struggling. I always admired my mom for her struggle. You know the story, a Black woman working several low-paying jobs just to make ends meet while raising four children whose father is a non-contributing alcoholic. As a child, I always thought, "I could never be half the woman that she is." I admired her for never letting us see her sweat. Through it all, she smiled easily, was always gentle, giving, and eager to learn new things. My mom and all of those who walked before us, have paved the road that we now walk on and I realize that my mother would be thrilled at the thought that, as a result of her work and the work of others, my path has been made smooth.

They showed us how to work hard, how to endure, how to make the impossible possible. They left us with all of the tools. Now, we have the luxury of using those tools to innovate. We can build highways and skyways. Rather than repeat their journey, I believe they would want us to start where they left off. We have their permission to soar!

CHAPTER 5

CREEPY CRAWLER OR WINGED BEAUTY?

If you change the way you look at things,
the things you look at will change.

—*Wayne Dyer*

I could see her face reflected back at me through the huge mirrors that hung on the four sides of all of the columns in the giant room.

My 5th-grade class had taken a field trip to a newspaper company, I think. I was mesmerized as I gazed at her face. I could not hear a word the tour guide was saying. How could this be? I was staring at her through the mirror and she did not hurt my eyes.

See, I could not look at my own face in a mirror. I was so ugly that looking at myself in the mirror hurt my eyes. But here I was, staring at her through the mirror, and my eyes didn't hurt. But, she was ugly too! She was even uglier than me (by our silly childhood standards)! She barely had any hair on her head. Her face was all scarred up; well, even her arms and legs were scarred. She was dirty. And she appeared so beaten down that her body language simply said, "Okay, I am ugly. I know it."

Now I was perplexed: I had assumed that ugly reflected back in a mirror is what made my eyes hurt, but now I am seeing that this is not true. So, if it wasn't because I was ugly, then why did my eyes hurt when I looked at myself in the mirror?

I came to realized that whatever it was that hurt me so deeply that I was unable to face myself was not external at all, but rather something internal. I knew that I needed to delve deeper into myself to get to the bottom of the problem. That day set me on a lifetime journey of constant self-analysis and self-reflection.

I needed to get to the bottom of why I felt so ugly, why I hated myself so much, why I was always so sad, and what, if anything, could I do about it. I voraciously read anything that I could get my hands on that seemed to be geared towards self-help. I watched people and I listened, grabbing any lessons from them that I could glean and make my own. I became a master in cause and effect. I learned to easily make connections between people's actions and the eventual outcomes. And, soon I could accurately predict what would happen next.

I figured out the answers to most of my questions. I knew why I felt ugly, hated myself, and was so sad. I even knew the generic answer that people gave for how to change all of that—"Love yourself," they said. The problem was that no one ever told you how to do that. When you hated yourself, how do you go about loving yourself?

I did all of the suggested things. I wrote extremely detailed journal entries for years. I spent time alone. I spent time in nature. I forced myself to look at myself in the mirror every day. I know that all of these things helped me along my path towards mental health. But it proved to be a long, slow process.

What I noticed all of those years ago is that things *are not* always what you think they are. What I notice today is that things *are* always what you think they are. I knew that I had a terrible aversion to seeing myself in the mirror. I thought it was because I was too ugly. As it turned out, I wasn't ugly after all! Ha! But what if I had never seen my classmate's face in the mirror? How much more of my life would I have spent as an "ugly" person (and how much longer would it have been before I realized I had some internal work to do)?

Whatever we believe to be true, will be true for us even if all of the world around you sees otherwise. If you think you are not smart, everything you notice in your environment will support that thought. If you think you suck at relationships, you sure will. If you think you can never do anything right, you will see yourself failing at everything you attempt. It's kind of like that new car phenomena—when you get a new car, all of a sudden, you will see hundreds of other cars out there that look just like yours. Those cars had been there all along, but you didn't notice them because your attention was elsewhere.

Self-proclaimed failures do things well, but they only see the things they do poorly.

I saw a demonstration at a Tony Robbins event that went something like this:

"Is there someone in the audience who cannot catch a ball? I mean, you just cannot catch. You wouldn't be able to catch a ball if your life depended on it."

Tony Robbins picked an eager hand to come up on stage.

"Let's see if you are telling the truth," he said as he threw the lady the tennis ball.

She was running all around the stage to retrieve the ball that he threw several times and she missed several times.

"Yep. You are right. You cannot catch a ball," he said. "But while you are up here, I want you to help me with something else. There is a big black X drawn on the ball. When I throw the ball, tell me which way the X is facing. Tell me if it is on the top of the ball, the bottom, the left side or the right side."

"Ok," she said.

As he threw her the ball, she focused her attention in order to provide Tony Robbins with the information he requested.

"The X was facing me," she said as she threw the ball back to him.

He tossed the ball again.

"The X was on the right side," she said as she tossed the ball back to him.

The audience had started to giggle.

"The X was facing me again," she said with the next toss, curious now because the laughter of the audience had grown much louder.

"The X was on the bottom," she said as she tossed the ball back the final time now looking around to try to understand what was so funny.

"Do you realized that you just caught the ball four times in a row?" Tony Robbins asked.

"Oh, my!" she exclaimed. "I promise you that I never caught a ball before in my life!"

"Do you know why you caught this ball four times in a row? Because you focused your attention on it. You had to look at the ball in order to tell me where the X was. The problem was never that you couldn't catch a ball. The problem was that you didn't know where to look. You just have to keep your eye on the ball."

I would submit that that is usually the problem, whether we are talking about balls or jobs or relationships or dreams. If there is a problem, it's not because you are incapable of it. It's because you don't know where to look.

The good news is whatever we believe to be true, will be true for us even if all of the world around you sees otherwise. If you think you are smart, everything you notice in your environment will support that thought. If you think you have great, loving relationships then you are surrounded by romance and good friends and family. If you think you are successful at everything you do, guess what? You will be.

Things *are not* always what you think they are **and** things *are* always what you think they are. Use this sentence to open yourself up to the possibility that just because you *know* you possess some trait that you do not desire, it doesn't necessarily mean that it is true. It could mean that you are looking in the wrong place. Use this sentence to also open yourself up to the possibility that you can choose to think whatever you want to think, and then that thought will become your reality.

⊷⊶

These ideas hold true whether we are talking about an individual or about a society or about the totality of humankind. If I had taken a snapshot of when I thought of myself at my worse and then used that picture to paint my future, I would have been wrong. I was (and continue to be) in a process of evolving. I continue to get better every day. I see the world like this too. We often lament about how terrible this world has become—the wars, the hungry children, the racial injustice that spreads across the globe. It's a dog-eat-dog kind of world. Take a snapshot of this and everyone would agree, it's not a pretty picture.

But if we look at the world like it is in a process of evolving, we can point out many improvements in the fabric of our consciousness over time. There is a growing tolerance around the world for people who are different from you; countries work together to develop cures and help eradicate disease and hunger; there is a greater focus on protecting our ecology.

The idea of evolution is really a beautiful thing. The desire to be better today than yesterday seems to be an inherent virtue in everyone. And not only do we desire this for ourselves, but we also are vested in ensuring that our children are even better still.

This inborn desire shows itself in many ways. Perhaps the most obvious display in our modern society is in the field of technology. The new and improved gadgets are rendered obsolete almost as soon as they hit the shelves. The race is always on for making every product better, faster, and more efficient than ever before. I remember the days when being able to see the person you are talking to on the other end of the phone or flying cars were simply fantasies. Since that time, so much has changed that it can make your head whirl.

Even aside from technology, most companies have had to evolve over time or risk the likelihood that the company would die. People drive the evolution of things. People imagine something yet undone, and then we do it. We make it a reality.

My personal evolution usually takes the forefront of my mind. When I am unkind, afraid, unmotivated, angry, sad, or even sick, I examine what is behind my mental distress and I look for ways to correct whatever faulty thinking I may be having. When I surprise myself at my level of compassion or patience or graciousness, I look for cues that help me to understand how I reached such an elevated state, and I make note to do that thing more often. Similar to a bud pushing itself out of the dirt into the sunlight and then radiating magnificent beauty, I push myself to bloom where ever I am and as often as I can.

I love the saying. "As above, so below, as within, so without, as the universe, so the soul."—Hermes Trismegistus. I use this idea as my barometer for testing my logic. If I know a phenomenon to be true on one level, then I presume it to be true on another level.

So, if I know that we are continuously evolving as individuals, then it only makes sense that the human race is also evolving. I can shift my focus just a bit and rather than see each person as an individual organism within the human race, I see the entire human race operating as one organism.

I know, for example, that there was a time when I was totally in the dark. I didn't see any beauty in myself. I then began a life-long search in order to get better and better. It is true that I sometimes get frustrated with myself when I don't change or improve quickly enough, but I don't allow myself to get stuck there. I have faith in myself and I trust the process. I know the direction that I am headed, so I keep moving. Like a caterpillar, I shed my old skin when it no longer fits and I meet the world on new terms.

I, therefore, conclude that the whole of the human race is doing the same thing. When I look at the world through this bigger lens, I trust that all of the ugly that I may see in the world is just a part of the process. Looking at any one moment in time might suggest that things are getting worse. But the overall push is for continued improvement.

When I take a look at "what is" with African Americans, I can see how unjust treatment seems to keep us spinning in a cycle that drastically slows our forward momentum. Similar to how I react to myself when I am falling short of my goals and ideals, I allow myself to be frustrated at the injustice and the resistance to growth and change. But, I don't allow myself to get stuck there. I have faith in us as humans and I trust the process. I look in the direction that we are heading and I continue my march forward.

I recognize that who we see ourselves as today (as individuals, as a race or all humankind), does not equal who we will see ourselves as tomorrow—a metamorphosis could be one thought away.

CHAPTER 6

HELD IN BONDAGE BY THE MIND

Wanna fly, you got to give up the
sh** that weighs you down.

—Toni Morrison, *Song of Solomon*

D o you think it is possible that you can change your
world by simply changing your mind? Can a different thought create a different reality? Can putting a new
meaning on something change the entire experience of a
situation?

This may sound strange to you, but when I was a kid, I
didn't understand that most things that were broken could
be fixed. Sure, if I pulled the arm or head off my dolls,
maybe it could be put back together. Or maybe certain

items could be glued back together or you could fiddle with the wires of electronics and get them working again. But, at my house, if a window was broken, it stayed broken. Or if a table lost its leg, then the table was no longer useful. If the door knob came off, then you use a screwdriver to open the door instead.

What I was failing to realize was that someone had actually made the item in the first place. Someone had a need and then thought about how to get that need met. They pictured the thing in their mind and then created it, often times, piece by piece. If it can be created once, then it can be created again. And rather than throw out the entire table, you could opt to fix the broken leg.

But the point is that thoughts produce things. Every broken item in my house was created twice—once in someone's mind and then again in its physical form. Thoughts produce other things too. When I think about this simply decadent, divine lemon cheesecake that I had once in New Orleans, my mouth begins to water. And my eyes quickly overflow with tears when I think about innocent children deserving of our utmost care who have been mistreated or neglected instead. And, just the thought that I might have to stand up to talk in front of a group of people makes my blouse wet right around my armpits.

I also realize that sad thoughts make me sad. Happy thoughts make me glad. Inspirational thoughts inspire me. And my "woe is me" thoughts make me, well, woeful.

Guess what else? If you say, "It is cold in here," I suddenly get cold. If you say, "I'm tired," then you better believe I am about to start yawning.

A thought is a mighty thing, isn't it?

It only takes one person to think of an idea powerful enough to send a man to the moon or to put a computer in every pocket or to ensure equal rights for all. By the same token, a thought can be the match that spreads hate, mistrust, greed, and fear like a wildfire.

Big businesses know how to leverage the energy of a thought. They make us feel fearful or that we are lacking something, then they tell us how their product will make everything better. Or, they present us with some desirable outcome—more popular, more stamina, more health or love—then they tell us just how successfully their product will elevate our status.

These days, there are all kinds of fascinating research being done on the power of thoughts to effect the world around us. Some of my favorite experiments include those done by Lynne McTaggart and those done by Dr. Masaru Emoto.

Lynne McTaggart studied the power of the mind to effect the physical world. In one study (that she later repeated 5 more times), she worked with the University of Arizona's Psychology Department. The university provided her with photographs of 4 sets of seeds with 30 seeds in each set. At one of her conferences, a group of about 700 people sent intentions to the photograph of a randomly selected set of seeds. Not knowing which set of seeds the intentions were sent to, the scientists planted all of the seeds and then measured their growth 5 days later. In all studies, the seeds that were sent the intentions grew higher than the seeds that had not been sent intentions.

The works done by Dr. Emoto with water crystals is quite fascinating too. He and his research team did a variety of experiments where they observed frozen water with a microscope. Much of their work was done using distilled water that they exposed to a variety of conditions. For example, they may have played music to the water, prayed over the water, or "shown" pictures to the water. They found that water that had been shown good words like "love", "beauty", "gratitude", or "peace" formed beautiful crystals. Beautiful crystals were also formed when the water "listened" to beautiful music or pure prayer. However, when the water was shown words like "hate" and "anger" or when water "listened" to rock music, the water either failed to form crystals or it formed incomplete or disfigured crystals.

With the human body being composed of over 80% water, Dr. Emoto's experiments make me think about how significantly our environment could affect us as individuals. If we are getting toxic messages all day long, either from ourselves or the world around us, how different is our chemical make-up from if we are receiving positive, loving messages all day long?

Lynne McTaggart's experiments make me think of the effect of huge amounts of people thinking the same way. For example, the picture of lack and hardship and unfair treatment and struggle is, not only the way that we as African Americans see ourselves, but it is also the way that others see us. With over 300 million people in our country thinking the same thought, it is enough to hold that thought in place.

Once we truly understand the potency of thoughts, it becomes clear that if we want to create circumstances that serve us better, then we have to be open to seeing things in a different way and to switch the focus of our thoughts.

Rather than accept our current thinking and current reality, we get to create a new picture that is painted with brighter, more vivid colors—colors of our own choosing. We get to decide on the splendor of our masterpiece.

⊷ ⊶

"If you believe it, you can achieve it."

"You can do anything that you put your mind to."

These are statements that have been floating around in our psyche for as long as most of us can remember. We have heard this idea repeated many times over. We may have even said it ourselves to our children when they are feeling defeated or even to a friend who is feeling discouraged. I think on some level, we all know this to be true. We know that when our backs are up against the wall, we are going to come out swinging. We know that when we hit rock bottom, we have no choice but to rise back up. We know "how to make a way out of no way."

It is in our nature as humans to believe in the possibilities and to believe that things can and should get better. It is this belief that caused the ending of slavery, that allows each of us to walk around with a computer in our pocket, and that gives us access to almost the entire world with the touch of a few buttons.

I, along with my business partner, Nin Aseeya, started an African-centered private school for toddlers to 8th-grade students. We offered the teachers a starting salary that was about $5000 higher than the public schools around us. The classes had 4-10 students each and most classes had a teacher and an aid. We provided our teachers with free lunch each day and an excellent benefits package. We purposefully made the environment as welcoming, homey, and peaceful as we could. We valued our teachers' input and acted on the suggestions that they made. But, it seemed that they still were not happy. They complained about every little thing and nothing was ever enough. I became frustrated.

"The more we give them, the more they want," I said. "They wouldn't even get half as much anywhere else."

"Oh no, I think it's a good thing," Nin Aseeya said. "We want to be the best school and they are pushing us towards excellence. The fact that they are asking for so much shows they are passionate about what they are doing and that they care. We should be worried if they *didn't* ask for more. They should always be asking for more."

Upon examination, I realized that what she was saying was true. That is our nature—to constantly seek improvement; to be better today than I was yesterday and to be better even still tomorrow. We want to grow, change, and create. And we want to set our children up to be able to rise beyond what we even dreamed of. We want them to know, too, that they can do whatever they put their minds to.

And, though I believe that we all believe on a gut level that "If you believe it, you can achieve it", I don't believe that the concept is real to us in our daily lives. I think that if we really believed that, then we would do more things and we would do things differently. I think that if we really believed that, we would paint a picture of what we really want and then commit to living into that picture. We would have vibrant health, loving relationships with our families, children and friends, and a quality of life where we could spend most of our time doing the things we love with the people we love. We would insist that no child was hungry and that every child gets a good education. We would ensure that our elderly, our mentally ill, and those who served our country well are getting their needs met. And, rather than see world peace as a pipe dream, we would make it so.

Instead, we are in a holding pattern. Yes, we work hard and take two steps forward, but you can almost be certain that you will then be faced with a major setback that leaves you close to where you started from. Maybe a tree fell on your house, or your car engine blew up, or a family member came down with a major illness. You make it through the crisis because, well, that's what you do. You know how to survive. Change is happening, for sure, but it is almost imperceptible. Today looks pretty much like yesterday. There is no real consistent momentum to get things moving in the direction that we want to move.

What stifles us? What keeps us from creating the lives that we want? Why do we settle for "good enough" when what we would love is right around the corner?

CHAPTER 7
OUT WITH THE OLD

Healing begins where the wound was made.

—*Alice Walker*

Thoughts, beliefs, and behaviors are intricately inter-mingled. Everything that we create starts first as a thought whether it is objects we can touch, emotions that we can feel, or behaviors that we can see. A thought created the atomic bomb as well as the sweet melodies that stir our souls. A thought created the fear of terrorist attacks as well as the ecstasy of being with the one you love. A thought created hate groups as well as groups that help grant wishes to our most vulnerable children. A thought is the precursor to creation.

Beliefs are our personally held thoughts. The bulk of our beliefs are simply handed to us from our families, from our neighborhoods, churches, and schools, from our cultural identity, and from our country of origin. The funny thing about beliefs is that the more important the belief is to you, the less able you are to recognize the belief. We are often not only blind to why we hold certain beliefs, we are also blind to the belief itself.

Whenever I had field trips at school, my mom would load me down with all kinds of foods to take with me. I would have several sandwiches, fried chicken, big bags of chips, cookies, candy, fruit and several frozen sodas wrapped in aluminum foil. I had to have enough of each thing to share with my classmates.

When I began going to college in Ohio, I immediately repeated the pattern of behavior of packing huge amounts of food for this 8-hour trip. Before one of my return trips home, I asked myself the question, "Why do I need to take so much food just to drive 8 hours?" I decided to just take a Granny Smith apple, some grapes, a bag of chips, peanut butter crackers and a big bottle of water—after all, I did want to keep my snacking options open. When I arrived home, I still had most of my food.

My mom was then preparing to ride with me back to school. "What foods should I pick up for our trip?" she asked.

"I was thinking we really don't need much," I said. Maybe just something to drink and a couple of sweet and salty snacks."

"Oh, I was going to make some sandwiches," she said.

"I figure that it's only an 8-hour drive. Why do we usually take so much food on the road for trips anyway? We never eat it?"

"Hmmm," she said. "That's a good question. I just thought that is what you are supposed to do. But now that you say that, you are right."

"Yes, let's just take some snacks. If we get hungry, we can stop on the road and buy something."

"Oh!" she said. "In my day, we couldn't stop on the road and buy something. Black people weren't allowed in many places. So, you had to be prepared. Besides, they didn't have all these fast food restaurants on every corner. Interesting, I never thought about that before."

It is our beliefs that hold our behaviors in place. Luckily for us, we don't have to think about what we believe before we take every single action. Most of that stuff is on autopilot. The problem arises when you want to change an old behavior or develop a new behavior but you have one of those beliefs in place that you are blind to. So, you continue to carry out the behaviors that support that belief, even though you so desperately want to change.

I was talking to a friend whose finances are in shambles.

"I want to have money. I want a little villa on the beach and to be able to travel and to eat fine foods. I want to have nice things and I want to be able to give my family the things that they want," she said. "My entire family has had problems with money. I am the one who has come the closest to being okay. But it has been a struggle."

"Well, a lot of times people want things but they have some underlying belief that they may not even be aware of that is holding them back. They may believe they are not deserving of money or that money is evil or...," my voice trailed off because I could see a light pop on in her eyes.

"Oh!" she said. "You just hit the nail on the head! I had forgotten all about this, but my brother was just talking about this the other night: My grandmother always said that a curse was put on our family. She said our whole family line was cursed and that we would never prosper financially. She paid good money to have someone to come to the house every month who was supposed to be removing the curse from our family. So, yes, I have always believed that we were cursed, but I had forgotten all about that!"

When I examine my own life, I can see that over the years, I have used a few different methods to change an old behavior or to begin a new behavior. I have often used pure grit and determination. This method takes lots of focus and discipline. And, sometimes, you can have the new behavior in place but as soon as you lose your focus, things can start slipping.

I was shaking my head because I had become disgusted with myself. Why was my closet in such disarray? Why hadn't I started writing my paper for class yet? When was I going to follow-through with making better food choices? I had told myself that I was going to do each of these things and much more. Yet, day after day, things were the same.

Although, if I gave my word that I was going to show up for someone else, it was as good as a done deal. I wasn't going to let anyone down. But I would promise myself that I was going to do this and I was going to do that, yet it seemed that nothing ever got done. I didn't believe myself whenever I told myself I was going to do something. Things had gotten so bad that whenever I told myself I was going to do something, I could almost hear my own voice laughing, saying, "Yeah, right." That is a sad situation to be in when you don't even believe yourself! Just a bunch of empty promises. It's worse than making plans with a friend who you know never shows up for anything. You have to live with yourself and live with the shame of knowing that you cannot count on you.

I decided to rename myself. My new name was Arvat Imma-do McClaine. And, I was going to be stuck with that name until I could do better. I forbade myself to give voice to anything that "I was going to do" until I had actually done it. I began writing what I was going to accomplish each day and I wrote beside each item the time that I was going to start it and my estimated finished time. I gave myself no other option but to do the task at the time prescribed. If I wasn't doing the task, then I didn't allow myself to do anything else either. My options were to either do the task or to stare at the wall until the task got done. In this way, I developed a new relationship with myself. I learned to be able to trust myself. My word to myself became my bond. I believed what I said and I worked to keep this trust in myself.

"I can do it! I can do it!" I emphatically said each time the manager of the housekeeping department told me she needed someone with experience.

"I need someone who can clean 13 rooms each day."

"I can do it! I used to clean my entire house and it had 9 rooms in it," I said a little because I was naïve but mostly because I knew I could successfully do whatever tasks that may lie in front of me.

"I need someone who is used to hard work and who doesn't need a lot of breaks."

"I can do it! I know how to work hard and stay focused," I said, determined to get this job.

"Besides, the job doesn't pay much."

"I can do it! I will even work for free for the first week. Then, if I can't do it, you don't have to hire me," I said.

Barely able to hide her amusement, the manager said, "I'm sorry. I can't hire you. I am really going to have to go with someone with experience because this is a really hard job. But," she continued, "here is the name and number of my friend who owns the gift shop downstairs. I believe she has an opening."

I was on break from school for the summer. I had gone to stay with one of my best friends from high school. She had gotten married and moved clear from Richmond, Virginia to Las Vegas, Nevada after our freshman year in college. Other than her new daughter and her husband's family, she did not have any real friends or anyone to talk to out there. When she invited me to Vegas that summer, I gladly accepted the offer.

In order to pay for the things that I needed to be successful in college, I had to work a full-time job during the summer months. But what I did not know was that most of the jobs in Las Vegas were union jobs. You had to be a part of the union to get one of these jobs, and I did not meet whatever the qualifications were to become a part of the union. I had been pounding the pavement looking for a job for well over 2 weeks. And in the Las Vegas heat, I would return home with a terrible headache every day. It was as if my brain were literally baking out there.

I knew I needed to get a job fast. When I left the house that particular morning, I promised myself that I would not return home without a job. At that time, there was only one hotel where you did not have to be a part of the union. That was Bob Stupak's Vegas World, and they were hiring housekeepers. If I did not get this job, there was a good chance that I would have to return home to Richmond, Virginia to get employment.

I went downstairs in the hotel to see the gift shop owner. Yes, she had interviewed a couple of people for the position and she had a few more to see. But, if her friend (the manager of housekeeping) had referred me, she would go ahead and interview me now.

At the end of the interview, she asked me, "Do you have any other questions?"

"Yes," I said. "When do I start?"

"Well, I still have a few other people to interview, but if I decide I want you, I will give you a call."

"Okay," I said. "When are you going to call me to tell me my schedule?"

Looking puzzled and seemingly not sure if I was having a problem comprehending what she was saying, she said, "I should know by morning."

I left that interview and I went straight home. I was so thrilled that I had gotten a job! When I told my friend what had happened, she had the same puzzled look on her face that the gift shop owner had.

Later that day, I called the gift shop owner. "Hello, this is Arvat McClaine. You interviewed me this morning."

"Yes," she said.

"I was just calling to see when you want me to report to work?"

She paused for a moment and then said, "Can you start tonight?"

Yes! I had both the power AND the courage! I had stepped totally outside of the person that I usually pretend to be (meek, scared, unable to make good things happen) and stepped into the person who I really am. I finally believed that I could do whatever I set my mind to do.

⊷⊶

I have had some success utilizing self-discipline and determination to power through to force myself to change my behaviors, but there is another method that I have used that proves to be a little easier than that. It is when something happens that interrupts my old thinking. Sometimes, another, more powerful idea or possibility can come along and disrupt my entire way of seeing things in an instant. Other times, I have had gradual shifts in my thinking, but in the long-run, a new thought replaced the old.

I was invited to attend a Ladies' Chat Night. The goal of the evening was to bring a group of women together to eat a little food, drink a little wine, and have a little fun while we do some *real* talk about issues that are important to us. In the room were 20 educated, articulate, upwardly mobile, fashionably dressed, gorgeous women. There were several business owners and a mixture of both blue collar and white collar workers. Many of the women had children, some married, some single. They ranged in age from 22-51. The women all seemed to be in a healthy place in the movement of their lives and dealing effectively with the drama that may show its head from time to time in life. But it was one area where they almost unanimously seemed to be challenged with getting a hold on—creating a healthy attitude around exercise and food. Throughout the evening, I heard two refrains repeated, "I am not motivated" and "It's a struggle". As such, 18 out of the 20 women were overweight.

Having struggled with my weight for many years, as I listened to the women, I hit rewind to remember how I had slipped so far in the weight loss battle and what I did to reign myself back in. The truth be told, I started my unhealthy relationship with food, my body, and weight long before there was even a hint that I would be overweight. I realized, that for me, the thought that I would be fat had been passed to me as easily as someone passes along the common cold. This thought was then allowed to incubate and had taken root in my psyche:

"I know we have been laughing and joking about your weight, but it really is a serious matter. You are too fat for your age. If you keep on like this, men are going to have a hard time keeping their hands off of you, so you'd better watch what you are eating," my favorite uncle told me.

I was 8 years old.

From that day forward, I became acutely aware of my body. I guess it really was my fault that male-folk couldn't keep their hands off of me. I was too fat. I began covering my body with long shirts and big sweaters.

"Am I too fat?" I would often ask my mom, siblings, and friends.

"No!" they would always tell me.

I really didn't look fat to myself either. But, over the years, I would keep receiving that message from outside sources so I figured it must be true.

My mom had big hips. Everywhere I went, people told me that I had those big hips just like my mom's.

All of my friends' mothers would tell me, "Girl, you got some big hips."

I remember my brother, Marcus, peering into our future and declaring that he and my younger brother, Scott, took after my dad so they were going to be thin. But my older brother, Raponyer, and I took after my mom, so we were going to be fat.

Then I met my mom's aunt—Aunt Queenie Mae. Aunt Queenie Mae had to be the spitting image except for an older version of my mom! I couldn't believe how much they resembled each other and their bodies were exactly the same! Hips and all. Looking at them, I could clearly see what my future held. The three of us were like generational stair steps. My fate was sealed. I just accepted it.

In an effort to conceal my fat body that would cause men to want to touch me, I continued to camouflage my body for years. Since my family had little material possessions, people from my church would often give us used clothes. I would select clothes that were a woman's size 12 to hide my 8-year-old body with its dangerous curves.

I eventually forgot that I didn't really wear a size 12, and continued to select size 12 clothing until my senior year in high school. I had gone to TJ Maxx to look at clothes with Harry, my then best male friend, now husband.

"Try these on," Harry begged as he held out the clothes that he had selected for me.

"No, I can look at those clothes and see they are too small," I said.

But he insisted. I went to the dressing room and slipped on the first outfit. Wow! It fit! I looked at the label to see the size. Size 8. They probably mislabeled these pants. But, who cares, they looked cute on me. I tried on the next outfit. Again, it fit! And, again, cute! What? Size 8? I was confused.

"They have the sizes all wrong because I wear a size 12," I said as I modeled the clothes for Harry.

"The sizes are right. You usually wear your clothes too big and even those clothes are too big," he explained. He wanted me to try on a size 6 to prove his point but I resisted and Harry left well enough alone.

From the age of 8 until the age of about 25, I thought I was fat although there was no real evidence to support that conclusion. Sure, I had ample buttocks and I was curvaceous but I was an average-sized female. Soon enough, though, I began to pack on some pounds, gaining a whopping 10 pounds every year! Having that extra weight caused a special kind of depression for me. Every time I looked in the mirror, I felt disgusted at what I had allowed myself to become. Every time I found the chair in my room piled with outfits that I had attempted to wear to work that day but discarded as a possibility because it looked awful on me, I felt pained. Every time I commented how the cleaners shrank my clothes, I quietly rolled my eyes at myself.

I knew that things had gotten out of control and that I needed to bring this weight gain to a halt. I tried a handful of diets but they never lasted for more than a week or two. I began exercising. Luckily for me, I never had an aversion for exercise, so I had more success in this department than dieting. But, even still, it was hard to be consistent for more than 3 or 4 months at a time. My life would get in the way.

Quite honestly, Oprah was the catalyst that jump started my consistent exercise program. When she finished her first marathon, 26.2 miles, I thought, "If she can do it, I can too." So, I signed up for my first marathon! Prior to my first day of marathon training, the only time I had ever run was in high school gym as required by the Presidential Physical Fitness Tests or as a kid playing games like kickball or Hide-n-seek.

It's been said that the journey of 1,000 miles begins with one step. On my first day of training, I squeaked out every bit of effort that I had to push my body to move around the track 4 times in order to complete a mile. I was feeling super-proud of myself when my coach said, "Now that you have warmed up, let's get started."

"Warmed up?" I said in shock. "I'm worn out!"

My coach took one look at my face and knew that I was serious. I could almost hear him say, "It is going to be a long road ahead."

But I was ready, and I was determined. See, I had also read Oprah's and Bob Greene's book, *Make the Connection*. The main idea that I had taken away from the book was the question, What is it going to take to get me to love myself so much that I will do whatever I need to do to accomplish my dreams and goals? I had repeatedly let life get in my way from getting my weight in check. Anyone else's crisis, big or small, was enough to derail my best efforts for exercising. But for me, my continual weight gain was a crisis too.

I knew that I would gladly go out of my way to assist anyone with anything. Why wouldn't I go out of my way for myself?

This simple question was enough to change my thinking and to help me create a new set of thoughts where I placed myself at the top of my roster of things to do. I got up before the sun came up each day and I ran over 600 miles during the course of training for that first marathon. And then, like Forest Gump, I never stopped running. In the process, I replaced the old image of myself as one who let life get in the way with a new identity—marathon runner.

Now, I know you are thinking that with all of that running that I lost that weight, right? Nope, sure didn't. True enough, it put a stop to the weight gain. I never gained another pound. But with all of that running, I never lost a pound either. I was still fat.

I remember years earlier, Janet Jackson had hit the scene with abs whittled to a perfect washboard. I eagerly sought out her magic formula for such a transformation. She had given up sugar. Oh. No chance in that for me. So, that piece of trivia went in one ear and then jumped out the window.

During the almost 20 years that I was overweight, I continued to try my hand at diets from time to time—seldom with any success. But I was making bold changes in my life in other ways. As a result of the new choices I was making, I completely and utterly fell in love with myself and with everything and everyone around me. My heart began beating with the rhythm of the universe. I began seeing myself in a new way. Rather than seething and feeling disappointed in myself every minute of the day for being fat and for being unable to do anything about it, I consciously visualized myself at the weight that I desired to be. I spent time each morning seeing and feeling how I imagined I would look and feel at that size.

By then, I had been doing a 10-day semi-fast at the beginning of the year for a few years. The first day of the fast, I would eliminate fried foods, sugar, and whites like breads, pasta, and rice. Each day, I would eliminate another food group like meats and fish one day, dairy the next, and finally fruits, until for the last few days, I would only be eating vegetables. Although this did take some degree of willpower on my part, it was a manageable fast.

The one benefit that I noticed after the fast was that after 10 days with no sugar, I would have lost my cravings for sugar. There would be no rush for me to eat my normal diet of candies, cookies, and cakes. But it wouldn't be long before I would eat those delicious treats again because it would be someone's birthday or some other reason to celebrate. And before I knew what happened, I would return to my habit of eating a few sugary snacks each day.

After spending months and months visualizing myself in a different way, I did the 10 day fast at the start of the year as usual. This time, I told myself that when the fast was over, I was going to wait until I actually *craved* sweets before I started eating them again. In other words, I was not going to eat the dessert out of habit or just because it was someone's birthday or another jovial occasion. I would only eat it if I really wanted it. I had no expectation as to how long I would end up going without sugar, but I definitely had no intention of depriving myself. And I wasn't looking to have Janet Jackson abs.

I wasn't too surprised when I made it through the first week without sweets because I knew my cravings would be gone. It was easy to walk past items that would normally cause my mouth to water. But, as the days went by, I became thrilled at each new milestone. Imagine me at 10 days with no sweets, 20 days, a month! I couldn't believe myself. I really wasn't even trying. There was no real effort on my part. I had simply followed my decision to not eat it unless I really wanted it. I had not really wanted it yet!

Then 40 days, 50 days, 2 months! Can you believe it? I still hadn't eaten any sweets! I felt like a million bucks for that accomplishment alone. But guess what? The pounds were falling off too! By the time I had hit the 3-month mark without sweets, I was at the weight that I had envisioned myself to be!

At about the 6-month mark, I changed my identity again. I was no longer someone who had taken it day by day and had gone half a year without sweets. I decided that my new identity was someone who does not eat sweets. Therefore, people didn't even bother to offer them to me and I no longer had to make a decision whether to eat it or not. With my new thinking about who I was, the decision had already been made. "No, thank you. I don't eat sweets."

During the years since that identity change, I have continued to make small improvements in my diet—just a tweak here and a tweak there. Each success built on the next. The whole process was easy! And, without any clear agenda or feeling of struggle on my part, my identity has evolved to one who definitely has her vices but who eats mostly healthy stuff most of the time.

There had been a full 11 years between the time that I had changed my identity from someone who lets life get in her way to a marathon runner and when I changed my identity from someone who couldn't get a handle on her diet to a person who did not eat sweets.

The confidence that I built in myself by knowing that my body (and my mind) could run over 26 miles opened the door for me to try each next thing. The first time it happened, it tickled me. My girlfriends and I were training for our upcoming triathlon (a swim, bike, run event). We were able to utilize a public pool to practice our swimming (or in my case, to learn how to swim). The pool manager assisted us by having all of the people who were just playing or wading in the pool to move to one side of the pool so that the lap lanes would be clear for our use. After swimming there a few times, when we would arrive, the people in the pool would say, "Clear the lanes. The athletes are here." Athletes? Now that was funny!!

It is true, running had become a passion of mine. To date, I have completed approximately 20 full marathons and countless shorter distances as well as 2 sprint distance triathlons and about 5 duathlons (a run and bike event). In addition, I enjoy hiking, yoga, kayaking, and participating in my daily outdoor fitness group (Seal Team PT). I even started 2 running groups. In general, people know to call me whenever they want to do some type of exercise activity, especially if it is an outdoor activity. But did I consider myself an athlete?

Well, I still don't think I am ready to claim the identity of an athlete. But I am happy with my current identity of being one who is healthy and fit.

⊨⊧

When I examine the elements of my journey with weight, some interesting pieces jump out at me. I can identify how the belief that I was going to be fat was formed. I can see how owning that identity closed off the possibility of being successful with a diet, exercise, or weight loss. Something disrupted or challenged my belief system or way of thinking. I created a new identity or belief about myself and lived into that new belief.

That pattern didn't just play itself out with my weight, I can pull example after example of this pattern in my life. For some beliefs, the change was slow like the weight loss. For other beliefs, change happened in an instant:

"Buck-toothed beaver!"

"Naw, she's got rabbits teeth!"

"You ugly!"

"Get away from me, you stink!"

On our way to the store one day, my two older brothers amused themselves by saying these and many other derogatory words to and about me as my younger brother listened. By this time, I was not only use to the insults, but I believed them all to be true. I had no fight left in me and I walked beside them in silence. They continued on.

"She looks like a roach."

"Naw, a cockroach!"

"Naw, she is nasty like a nasty fly."

Then, my younger brother, Scott, chimed in. For a moment, I was stunned and I felt betrayed. Although I always felt that he was in agreement with my brothers, he rarely joined in on their beat-Arvat-down sessions.

"A fly?" he said. "She's no fly! She is a butterfly!" And in that moment, I grew my wings, and I flew far, far away from there.

See, there it is again: I believed I was ugly, nasty, and no one wanted me around. Therefore, I exhibited behaviors to support my belief. I was powerless. I had no fight. I accepted my unworthiness. Something interrupted my pattern of thought or belief. The sweet words of my little brother made me realize that, at least to him, I was something special. So, I changed my behavior. I disregarded their opinions of me and I was free to create my own.

⋙ ⋘

The third method that I have used for creating change in my life is to utilize the creative power of thoughts as well as the creative energies in the universe that are available to all of us at any time. I started to become aware of these energies as a child although I wasn't exactly clear on what anything meant or the exact ingredients used in the recipe for change.

In the Yoruba culture, there is no word for "fiction" or "make-believe". They believe that if you can imagine it then you can bring it into existence in the physical realm. I believe this too. That is why I cannot watch scary movies of any kind. "It's not real. I don't know why you won't watch it," my friends who love scary movies tell me.

"If someone was capable of dreaming these scenarios up, then it is possible that this stuff can really happen," I give my standard response.

Though I was never a particularly religious person, I have always relied heavily on my faith in God. I also have had enough dips into the "unexplained" to let me know that there is more to this thing we call life than meets the eye.

From a wee bit of a child until I was well into my teenage years, one of my favorite things to do was to sneak into my mom's room and pull out of her dresser drawer her little white box. Inside the box was a necklace. It was a glass, heart-shaped pendant with gold trim on a gold chain. Inside of the heart was a very tiny mustard seed. Also in the box was a little strip of paper with the words, "He who has the faith of a mustard seed has the power to move mountains."

I would stare at the little mustard seed, close my eyes, and squeeze the pendant in my hand. I would think, "I have to have as much faith as this little tiny seed". I would envision myself making mountains move. Slowly, the huge mountains would move across the landscape of my mind.

When I was a kid, I use to possess a special little talent. I honestly and truthfully would often know things were going to happen before they actually happened. And, when they happened, I would say, "I knew that was going to happen!"

I also use to have frequent episodes of déjà vu. I would be so puzzled because I would be certain that I was repeating entire scenarios in my life. I would search my mind for ways to make it make sense. "Wait a minute," I would think. "I have already done this before. I have already said these words. I already know what is going to happen next. But... when? When had I done this before? How was this possible?" My mom finally explained to me that lots of people have this experience but no one knows why.

And, maybe, just maybe, I had the ability to make things happen with my words and my mind.

Two incidents happened back to back while I was in elementary school that brought me to that conclusion.

"We should stay home from school tomorrow," my upstairs neighbor said to me.

"Yea," I say. "How are we going to do that?"

"Let's pretend like we are sick," she said.

"Okay," I say.

I went to bed that night, a little excited as I practiced the lie I would tell, over and over in my head.

When I woke up the next morning, I had changed my mind. I was going to school. My mom touched my face and then said, "You are hot! Get me the thermometer."

I was sick. No school for me.

Of course, my upstairs neighbor went to school that day. When she returned home, she asked, "Why didn't you go to school?" "I am sick," I told her.

"No, you aren't! You lied!" she said.

I was too sick to even defend myself.

A day or so later, a mean boy at my school was doing what he always does. He was being mean! I was tired of him terrorizing everyone every day. I said to myself, "I hope he breaks his leg". The next day, he came to school in a cast with crutches. "Oops!" I thought. "Did I cause that?"

I thought about the lie I wanted to tell about being sick, and then I really was sick. I thought about the mean thought I had about the mean boy, and now he is on crutches. I prayed for forgiveness. From that day, I promised I would monitor my thoughts because I believed I had the power to make things happen with my mind.

Were those incidents coincidences or did I make things happen with my mind? I still do not know the answer to that question, but to this day, I will not tell a lie (unless it is about something that I actually want to happen), and I will not wish anything bad on anyone (no matter how much they may deserve it).

I remember in the early 70s, the television was turned on to a news-like talk show, perhaps "60 Minutes", and they started talking about ESP. I immediately tuned into what was being said because I had experienced many of the same phenomena that the people who were being interviewed had experienced. I watched with interest as people were validating what I had been experiencing and I believe they even had people on the show bending spoons with their minds.

After all had been said, a scientist, the final authority on the matter, explained everything that was happening away. It was not anything mystical at all. People with this so-called ESP were simply better at picking up on cues that were already in front of all of us. He gave explanations similar to: When you are humming a tune and then turn on the radio and that exact song is playing it is likely due to you being able to hear it ever so faintly playing on someone else's radio, or some people are just extremely good at reading other people's facial expressions and body language.

Whatever his explanations were, I bought in to them. I forgot all about that ESP nonsense.

In hindsight, when I think about what he was saying, although his intent seemed to have been to invalidate the experience of ESP, what he really said is this is a power that we all have. Some people are just better at tuning into the unseen energy field that we all are a part of.

But what if there is a way that we can all become better at tuning into that energy field? What if God really did make us in His image and equipped us with everything that we need? What if our time in our physical form, here on earth, was meant to be a playground for us—a time to experience pure joy rather than repeated hardships? What if by simply interrupting our current beliefs, we could replace them with beliefs that bring us more love, more joy, better health, better relationships, and the financial freedom to dream and create our biggest dreams?

CHAPTER 8
IT'S ALL IN YOUR MIND

*Never be limited by other people's
limited imaginations.*

—Dr. Mae Jemison

I was jumping around, screaming at the top of my voice, "Yes! Yes! I did it!" I high-fived the hands of the people around me as they, too, celebrated their own victories on a warm night in Georgia.

We each had just completed the fire walk at a Tony Robbins event. Yep, we actually walked barefooted across a burning bed of coals!

As surprising as that might sound, the truth is, I wasn't at all surprised that I had just willingly put the soles of my bare feet against the glowing red embers. See, Tony Robbins had thoroughly prepared us over the past few days to move past obstacles that may otherwise paralyze us. In his highly-charged seminar, he did a lot of talking, we did a lot of dancing, but the actual procedure for getting us prepared to walk across the coals was quite simple. He showed us how to program ourselves to believe that we could. (This is a very simplified version of our immersion experience. Find more information on the Tony Robbins website.)

Repeatedly, throughout the course of the seminar, I stood in my best Wonder Woman pose and I felt the feeling I imagined Dianna Prince would feel after she changed into her scanty yet powerful outfit and then successfully apprehended the biggest criminal in town—this was my power pose.

"Yes! Yes," I then jumped and shouted as I pumped my body and psyche up to take on the challenge ahead.

Then I would imagine myself walking smoothly and confidently across the scorching hot coals. At the end of my visualization, I literally go wild, jumping around in celebration as if I had actually physically completed the fire walk.

I had repeated this scenario so many times throughout the course of the seminar that by the time we went outside to actually walk across the coals, I already knew I could do it!

Just like I had practiced, I took my power pose, yelled "Yes!", walked smoothly across the coals, and then celebrated like crazy at the end of my walk!

A big part of what Tony Robbins had us do in order to overcome the fear that might be associated with walking barefooted across a hot bed of coals was to employ the use of *visualization*. Tony Robbins reminds us that the brain can't distinguish the difference between what is real and what is imagined. Similar to the Yoruba belief that if you can imagine it, you can achieve it, Robbins had us repeatedly imagine ourselves walking through our fears. If we can overcome the fear of walking across a hot bed of coals via visualization in one weekend, what can we move through in a week, a month, a year?

━━ ━━

While in undergraduate school at Randolph-Macon College, it became apparent to me that my fellow peers had received far more varied and rich educational experiences than what had been offered to me prior to my arrival at the college. I still did well in school, but witnessing how my peers took for granted the vast opportunities of their previous educational pursuits left me wanting the same for all children. My steps became ordered with the overriding purpose of creating a school environment where Black children, in particular (but all children, in general), could feel proud of being exactly who they are, be exposed to as many types of learning situations as possible, learn to be leaders, learn to express their creativity, develop a social and spiritual conscious, and become confident players in the game called life.

After graduating from Randolph-Macon College, I attended The Ohio State University because, at the time, it was one of only two universities in the country that offered a master's level degree in the area of Black Studies. While attending The Ohio State University, I learned all that I could about Black people from every aspect that I could.

In class, I learned about our history and about the different Black people all across the Diaspora. I studied our politics, music, language, art, culture. I studied our economics, psyche, parenting. I studied our relationships with each other, with the opposite sex, with other races. I studied our learning modalities, methods of expression, creativity. In the city of Columbus, I studied community building, African dance, social interactions. One of the best lessons that I learned in the community at the African Center was the dynamics of Black men and Black women relationships. I credit the African Center with teaching me how to be in a relationship with a Black man. I attended conferences and conventions and read books and I learned and learned and learned about what it means to be a Black person living in America.

Next up was to pursue a doctorate in Urban Education from Old Dominion University. In the same way that I inhaled everything that was "Black", I absorbed all that I could about the best ways to educate a child. Every paper that I wrote at Old Dominion University, in some form or fashion, was directly related to this school for Black children that I was preparing myself to start.

Almost a year later, in the summer of 1995, my husband, Harry, was offered a job at another company very similar to the one he was already doing except with a higher rate of pay. When Harry went to resign from his job, his job asked him to stay on with them and they offered him a pay increase that he could not refuse.

"Don't you see, Harry? This is exactly why you have to refuse," I said convincingly. "They want you and they want you bad! You are providing something for them that they need."

"What?" he said. "I'm just doing my job."

"I don't know," I said. "But they know."

Right then and there, I started interviewing Harry, asking him specifically what his job entailed and asking him if it were his company, what would he keep the same and what would he do differently. I asked him to dream his biggest dream if that were his company.

As he spoke, detailing his day to day experiences and how he could make that company great, I began formulating a clear picture in my mind. That night, as most of our city slept, I designed our first company brochure detailing everything that Harry had expressed to me.

The next morning, I excitedly showed Harry the brochure.

"Wow! This is nice. Uhm... are we starting a business?" he asked.

"Do you want to?" I said. "What's the worst thing that could happen?"

"We could fail," he said.

"Do you feel confident that if the business doesn't work out that we could still get back on our feet?" I said.

"Yes," he said. "Let's do it!"

Within a couple of weeks, armed with only a computer and a fax machine, H.W. Renaissance, Incorporated was officially in business, providing services for at-risk youths and their families.

Harry's previous company was right. He definitely had that "thing" that was needed. I called it magic. So, I went about developing the structure and the programming and Harry waved his magic wand that brought everything to life. Together, we went about striving to provide top-notch care for not only our clients but for our employees too. In this manner, our business continued to grow. Each year, we took our total profits and divided it right down the middle. Fifty percent of our revenues would be divided evenly in the form of a raise for our employees. We invested the other 50% into purchasing real estate. Though we were technically cash-poor, with this process, we became financially independent before we had reached our 35th birthdays.

By providing over 90% of the funding, our company helped to make my dream of starting a school (along with co-founder, Nin Aseeya Ra-el), Nubian Village Academy, come true.

While operating our company definitely had its rewards, the major problem was that we worked too long and too hard never with any relief in sight. We became physically, mentally, emotionally, and spiritually drained. We worked ourselves until we were just shells charading as people.

There were many times when I would work all day and evening at the school and then go straight to the group home to work all night and then go straight to the school to work all day. Often, without having the opportunity to drive the 5 minutes to my centrally located home, I would have on the same outfit for 2 days in a row.

"Dear God, please relieve me of some of this burden," I pleaded consistently. "Please send me somebody who can tell me something. I need someone wiser than me to guide me."

There were so many times when I just wanted to quit— throw in the towel. But, I would hear whispered to me words that a friend told me at the very start of our company, "We need you to continue to exist."

With that, I would muster up some strength from deep down inside, and I would ensure that we continued to "exist" for a little while longer.

As part of our ongoing personal development, Nin Aseeya and I would choose a book to read and discuss each month. We quickly came upon a little book that I credit with elevating my life to the next level, *The Seven Spiritual Laws* by Deepak Chopra. I found the book to be such a jewel that we made it part of the mandatory training program for all personnel at the school. As I reviewed the book over and over again with all new employees, the ideas of the book became a part of me.

The idea in Chopra's book that I initially understood the least but that has the greatest impact on how I currently spend my days is the Law of Least Effort—doing less and accomplishing more. I have always understood and believed in the value of hard work and giving something your total energy to ensure its existence and survival. As a matter of fact, our company motto was, "We are used to hard work and we are used to success." But, I have come to realize that when my intentions are pure and my total being is lined up with my desire, the entire universe seems to respond in an effort to bring to me exactly what I want. It does not always mean that I do not have to work for it, but, rather the work feels less like hard work and more like joyful work. When things begin to feel hard, I have to put on the breaks and reassess my intentions, my desires, and my spiritual health.

This new understanding helped me to reevaluate my intentions with our business. I had become so short-sighted, stressed, and bottled up that I was asking for relief for myself. But I had not wanted to do this business for my own personal comfort. I had wanted to do this business in order to provide loving, nurturing environments that would inspire the children we served, our employees, and all helping agencies with whom we interacted.

Armed with clarity, rather than ask God to relieve my burdens, I borrowed the sentiments from the "Prayer of Saint Francis". "Dear God," I prayed, "make me a channel of *Your* love. Make me a channel of *Your* peace." And I would visualize God's love pouring into me as I radiated that love out to the entire world.

And, guess what? My life did begin to change.

⇒⟨⟨ ⟩⟩⇐

It was in the summer of 2002 when Harry and I spent 14 days on this tiny little island—21 miles long, 15 miles wide—Barbados. Sun so bright that it burns your skin, deserted white sandy beaches, and water, a blue so rich that it touches your core. Fourteen days of this! Fourteen of the longest, most boring days of my life!

Every day, I would count, again, how many days we had left before we would be returning home. Argh! How could time move so slowly? See, I was so used to moving at the speed of light and being totally consumed by everyone's concerns and issues, that to actually stop and be quiet was unthinkable! For me, it was not possible. I needed to get home! But since Harry seemed to be enjoying himself, rather than shout, "Let's blow this camp!" at the top of my lungs, I just whispered, "And, how many days do we have left here?" each and every day.

84

We did at least one touristy thing every day like go parasailing or snorkeling or getting on the submarine. We ate the local foods, participated in the local festivities, and took tours of places of interest.

At the top of every morning, I walked out of the hotel on a trail that took me to the beach. Even that early, the sun was already hot on my skin. I would walk down about a mile to the end of the beach. I walked on the wet sand close to the water's edge. Occasionally the water would roll in higher and faster than I expected and it would cause me to run and laugh at my efforts to escape it. I would then sit on a huge log that had found itself stranded on the beach and I would attempt to meditate. With closed eyes, a slow deep breath in and slowly out—1; slow breath in and slowly out—2; in and out—3.

Before I knew what happened, I was thinking about all of the things to be done back home at work. Every day, I would make repeated attempts to just make it to 10 deep breaths in. I could not focus long enough to get past 3.

Finally! We were on the plane; we buckled our seat belts. Richmond, here we come! I was excited! As the plane began to lift off, I turned to look out of my window. A rainbow! A beautiful, brilliant rainbow. I began to cry, "Harry, I don't want to go! I want to stay!"

Back at home, it was business as usual. The race was again on. We began thinking about getting out of the business.

We put our company on the market to be sold. Our selling agent advised against us actually meeting the people who had interest in buying our company, but we insisted. We declined offer after offer because each person came in saying the same thing. They wanted our company because they wanted to make money. Obviously, that is a reasonable desire, but we were unwilling to sell to someone who did not rank the well-being of our clients as their top priority.

We decided on a new route—hire an Executive Director. Soon (maybe too soon), we were out of the door. We were heading back to Barbados; this time for a 6-month sabbatical!

We had secured a place to reside from October 2003-March 2004, or so we thought. Literally, a couple of days before we were scheduled to leave Richmond, our living arrangements fell through. A quick internet search landed us at a charming seaside villa at the very most southern tip of the island. We figured we would stay there for about 2 weeks or until we found a more long-term placement.

We simply fell in love with that part of the island. Being on the southern tip of the island gave it several remarkable features. Because of how Barbados is situated, the West coast of the island is largely influenced by the calm, Caribbean Sea. Most of the tourists are drawn to the peaceful waters of the West coast. The East coast of the island is largely influenced by the fiercer Atlantic Ocean. The water on the East of the island is good for surfing. But the South coast, where the two bodies of water intermingle, have characteristics of both. The waters are not too rough and not too calm. The South coast also gets a consistent breeze that almost 100% of the time blows from the East.

But there are two traits of the south coast that we love the best. The first is that we can watch the sun rise from the East, seemingly from out of the ocean in the mornings and watch the sun set in the West back into the ocean in the evenings. The other is that, because the water here is not the calm, wading water, nor the rolling waves needed for surfing, few tourists frequent this area, therefore, we get to have our own private beaches.

We ended up finding a place about a block from the ocean and about 3 blocks from the coziest little beach that we call "Our Beach".

My daily routine quickly becomes set. I leave the house while it is still dark. I run about 1.5 miles down to the popular Miami Beach taking the road closest to the coastline so that I can hear the waves upon the shore. I return to the southernmost cliff of the island in time to watch the perfect sun rise out of the ocean, a different view every day due to the infinite positioning of the clouds. There, the breeze prompts me to deeply breathe in probably the freshest air available. The ocean spray mists and cools my hot and already wet from sweat skin. I watch the waters ebb and flow and the turtles blithely come up for air. It is here that I begin to feel the pulse of the universe. It is here that I begin to realize that that pulse is my own, as well as the pulse of everyone and everything that exists.

I run home to collect my composition book where I have recorded my heart's desires and CDs from some of our current-day spiritual teachers. I listen to the CDs as I walk to a hidden, little-known place on another cliff. There, with uninterrupted focus, I visualize all of the things I want in life—loving relationships, perfect health, lose weight, be a philanthropist, travel.

Later that day, I play in the ocean and then I watch the sun temporarily leave us to shine light on someone else's day.

I learned and changed a lot that fall and winter (which seemed like an endless summer to me), but we were called home earlier than planned. Our business was taking a nose-dive. We had to get back immediately or there would be no business to which we could return. In the midst of working to get the business back on track, tragedy struck. One of our clients, 14-year-old Donny, drowned in the James River while in our care. His death had a devastating effect on the hearts of everyone in our agency.

We were able to assist the people in our agency through the loss and to resume business as normal. But our hearts had suffered a major attack. Neither Harry nor I wanted to continue this work that we had poured our everything into. We decided that we wanted to close the business but we wanted to close it on a good note. So, we set the date— by Christmas 2005, we would be living in Barbados. And, similar to starting from scratch, we re-built our business, only this time, we simply followed the recipe that we already had in place.

⚒

The rainbows, the lighthouse, the monkeys, the sun, and the ocean! We were back! Back to this place we were planning to call home for the next 5 years.

We were lucky enough to move back into the exact apartment that we had stayed in before. And the daily routine had a face very similar to the routine I had before— the runs, the sun, the cliffs, the quiet time alone in nature. Only, I did not feel the same ecstasy and connectedness as before. Rather, I felt cold and disconnected.

On the cliffs, I met a Bajan fellow named Carl. He would always arrive on the cliff before I did to watch the sun rise out of the sea. Carl was a small, quiet, pensive sort of guy with dreadlocks that hung past his shoulders. He loved Barbados and he loved to share with me the customs and the distinct features of their little island. He pointed out fruit on trees and told me the names and uses for the various plants.

He did not know everything.

"Hey, Carl, what kind of birds are those?" I said pointing to the black birds that frequented the island.

"We call those the black birds," he said.

"What kind of birds are those?" I said, pointing to the tall white birds that stayed on the cliffs closest to the shore.

"We call those the white birds," he said.

"Oh," I said, trying hard to be as serious as he seemed.

But, he was quite wise.

"The reason that you are not feeling connected is the same reason that any Bajan person could take one look at you and know that you are from the States," he explained to me in his heavy Bajan dialect. "It's because you have ice," he said.

"Ice?" I said

"Yes, you have ice in your skin. I can see it. Once you are here for awhile, your ice will melt. Then you will be like me, like a Bajan."

Thinking back on my previous visits to Barbados, I remembered the initial feeling of restlessness and then, yes, the melting. I went from being *in* Barbados to being *of* Barbados.

And, he was right. It took about a month for the process to be complete, but this time, too, my ice did melt, and it was as if the make-up of my cells had totally changed.

We lived a very simple life while on the island. We opted to not have a vehicle while on the island because not having a vehicle would force us to immerse more fully in the culture of the island. But to get anywhere, we had to walk about a mile to reach the bus stop where we would board a van, designed to carry 12 passengers, that sped through the streets with blaring music, often teetering from the weight of the 16 or more passengers crammed on the van at a time.

I rarely ever ventured out of the house between the hours of 10 am to 4 pm because the sun was just too hot. In order to survive the heat, contrary to my rational thinking, I was taught that I needed to put on more clothes instead of fewer clothes.

I loved the fact that during working hours, Bajans, particularly the women, were always impeccably dressed, complete with pantyhose, blazers, three-inch heels and smelled of some divine fragrance. Yet, it still was not out of the ordinary for either the call of the blue waters or the unmistakable heat to overtake them. While walking past the ocean, the women may strip out of their clothing for a quick sea bath. The men would sometimes jump in the ocean, just for a quick dip, clothes and all.

Other than my morning and evening outdoor rituals, I had time to do a few other things during the day. I used that time to catch up with family and friends via the internet. I thought it was so cool that both mine and Harry's moms purposefully and willingly extended their knowledge of the computer and using the internet so that we could stay in daily contact. I had long philosophical email conversations with friends. And, I was able to simply tell others that I loved and missed them. This was so important to me because, for the previous 10 years, I had worked to the neglect of everyone and everything outside of work. So, renewing relationships that I had abandoned meant the world to me.

I also had time to earn a doctorate degree in Parapsychic Science from the American Institute of Holistic Theology. I had come full-circle. Although I had an interest in this area as a child, I spent most of the following years believing that if it cannot be proved by way of science, then it must not exist. But, I could never deny the abundance of instances in my life that have occurred that had no possible current-day scientific explanation.

Another one of the things that I loved doing was being a part of Westside Toastmasters. Because I wanted to improve my public speaking skills, I did an internet search to see if there was a Toastmasters club in Barbados. There were a few. I made contact in order to visit the various clubs. The first club that I went to was Westside. To get there, I had to walk a mile to the bus stop. Ride about 30 minutes on the overcrowded van to Bridgetown. Walk a block or two to find a taxi. Take about a 15-minute taxi ride to the club. Getting back was worse because now it would be dark. I would have to call and wait for a taxi and reverse the process.

"I loved your club but getting there and back is too much trouble. I need to find a club closer to me," I said when the club's president called me to see if I was interested in joining.

"If you can get here, I promise you that someone here will give you a ride home. We really want you to be a part of Westside Toastmasters," he said convincingly.

I decided to give it a try. I enjoyed preparing my speeches. I did not mind the time investment to get to the meetings. And the members of the club were marvelous! Each meeting, several people would ask me if they could give me a ride home. Nevertheless, I always felt anxious at the end of the meeting. I did not like not knowing who was going to give me a ride home before getting there. I was always taught that when you plan to go somewhere, you also need to plan for how you were going to get back. Nor did I like feeling dependent on other people.

"I really don't like having to depend on you guys for rides home," I said to my ride for the evening.

"Well," he said in his Bajan dialect, "you seem to me to be a very loving and giving person. I would imagine that you have spent your life doing for others. What we put out in the world, we get back. It may not be from the same people or in the same form that you gave it. But you will get it back. This is just you getting back a little of what you gave. It is give and take. Accept it. I love to be able to do this for you."

"Thank you," I said. My heart was smiling.

On the third Tuesday of each month, Harry and I would walk to the nearest hotel. We would have dinner at the outside restaurant on the oceanfront and stare up at the multitude of stars in the sky. There was one bright light that hung so low in the sky, more like on the horizon, that it seemed impossible that it could be a star.

"No, there are not more stars in the Barbados sky," said the astronomer who brought his fancy telescopes to the hotel one Tuesday each month to help educate and entertain the hotel guests. "There is just much less ambient light here, so it just appears as so."

Though we became regulars to his sky tours, we held on to his every word. And, we began to notice how the sky changed with the seasons. We loved to be able to see the actual gas rings around Saturn. And, that low star, Barbados is the highest point in the northern hemisphere where that star can be seen. In other words, the star cannot be seen from the United States because the United States is too far north to see the star.

I would amuse myself by watching animals which amused themselves by watching me. I had a habit of running up and down a steep hill near my house just before the skies would begin to lighten to suggest a new day. I would run to the top, back to the bottom, back to the top, and repeat ad nauseam. I would hear the trees begin to sway as if a hard wind was blowing. By about my third time up the hill, I would see that clans of monkeys had gathered to watch me from the perch of the trees. I would always greet them with a cheery, "Good morning" and wonder what they were thinking of this strange human behavior.

Also, there were two black birds which I passed each day on my travels that lived about a mile apart from each other who were either partial or impartial to me. I was never exactly sure which. The one that lived closest to my home would charge back and forth at my head coming so close and so fast that I would duck and hide my face for fear that one day he would actually attack me. The other lived near a cliff where I sat each day to meditate. He would meet me at the entrance-way and dart back and forth from one side of me to the other as I walked towards my resting place. He would then sit there with me for a while; fly off for a while, and then periodically return as if to check to see if I was okay.

Oh, and the rainbows! How could I forget the rainbows? I always felt that the rainbows were a special treat for me and the rainbows seemed to love me back because they appeared before my eyes on such a regular basis. They would be so vibrant with no two ever looking exactly the same. Often there would be double rainbows. One day when Harry and I were in the ocean, the rainbow appeared. To our utter amazement, the beginning (or the ending) of the rainbow directed itself not even 10 feet away from "Our Beach".

Having to know if the age-old adage was true, "Harry get out of the water and go get our pot of gold!" I said

"Okay!" he said with enthusiasm. "Now what exactly am I looking for?"

"I don't know. Maybe there is an old coin or an ancient ring or anything like that. Just dig around," I said.

"I don't see anything," he said. "Am I digging in the right spot?"

"Move a little to the right," I yelled since from my distance I was better able to see the ending of the rainbow.

Well, we did not find our pot of gold but we sure have a funny story to tell. And, really, for us, the island was our pot of gold.

But more than anything, best of all was who I became sitting on the cliffs, absorbing the sun, and becoming one with the waves. I became infused with love overflowing. And I would visualize myself radiating this love out to the entire world.

⟞⟝ ⟞⟝

Over the years, I have used three different methods to change old behaviors or to begin new behaviors: I used brute willpower, or something interrupted my old thinking pattern in favor of something new, or I utilized the energy field that surrounds us every day. Each serves a purpose and has its place, but some techniques are much easier and have more predictability than others.

Using pure will power usually requires self-discipline, hard work, and sacrifice. When you have success here, it is wonderful, but when you can't seem to hold yourself accountable no matter how hard you try, you end up beating yourself up and feeling worse about yourself than you did before you tried to make a change. When my husband and I had our own business, there were entire years when I relied heavily on my sheer will and determination. I forced myself to keep going when I felt like I wanted to quit. I sacrificed relationships with my friends, my family, and myself because I had made a commitment to offer the best care to the children whom we served and I strove with all my might to do just that. In exchange for creating the company that I had committed to creating, I lost myself and felt physically, emotionally, and spiritually bankrupt.

I think behavior change is easy when something comes along and so completely interrupts your current thought patterns or challenges your belief system in a way that makes you feel that you would be crazy to keep holding onto your current ways of being in the face of this new information. The problem with this method is that you never know when or where you will come across something powerful enough to make you re-think everything. As a business owner, the idea that changed everything for me was the idea of becoming clear on my intentions. See, I had been asking God for help, but my prayers were almost in direct opposition to what I really wanted. I was praying that God take the burden off of me. But I never really wanted to offer less services nor less of myself. In actuality, I wanted to offer more. But I didn't feel that I had anything else to offer. I felt that I was giving my entire self away. Once I was clear on my intentions, I was able to ask for help in a new way. I was able to ask that I be connected to that unending flow of love so that I could pour more love out to more people.

This new prayer led me directly to the third method that I use which is by far the easiest and most predictable method to create the kind of life that you want—utilize the help that is already here waiting for our beck and call. Create what you want with your imagination. Visualize it and know that it is already true. In my new prayer, I could see, in my mind's eye, God pouring his love into me and I, in turn, radiated this love out to the entire world. I eventually found myself doing just that—radiating on the cliffs of Barbados (thereby positioning myself to serve many more people in a much different way).

CHAPTER 9
GETTING TO KNOW YOU

Challenges make you discover things about
yourself that you never really knew.

—*Cicely Tyson*

O
h, gosh! How did I let this happen again?! What was
I thinking? Let me get out of here!

Once again, it had happened. I just heard the screen
door slam as my brothers left our small but neat apartment
to go outside to play or to do who knows what.

At the same instant that I am realizing that I need to
get out of the house, my dad appears before me. He looks
at me the same way that he has looked at me many times
before, and I already know what is going to happen next.
I immediately put myself into my robot mode where I can
reside almost untouched and unphased by what is to come.

Almost, I say, because I can feel that little burning in my chest, and I just will it to go away.

I am guided to the sofa where I drop to my knees. He unfastens his pants and guides his penis into my mouth. I hold onto it with one hand. He pushes and pulls my head up and down as I work hard to not gag and to keep my eyes from bugging out of my head. Soon, I am transported from that space. I am in another world—floating—until I am brought back into this place; disturbed from my safe place because now he wants me to lie on the sofa.

He pulls my pants off. He tells me he will be right back. As I lie on the sofa waiting for his return, I am wondering if I should do something right now. Should I get up and put my pants back on? Should I run out of the house? Should I scream? Should I tell him I don't want to do this? But, I do nothing, but lie in wait. He returns. My excitement about possible escape is replaced by dread and an overwhelming disgust with myself for being unable to save myself when doing anything would certainly be better than doing nothing at all.

He parts my legs and begins gently and deliberately wiping my private parts with a damp washcloth. When I am clean enough, he begins swirling his tongue all over the parts that he has just wiped clean. I take a deep breath, and I hold it. Again, I am being transported from that place to a world just above it. But, he brings me right back.

He says, "Does that feel good?"

"Yes," I say.

He continues in the same manner. Again, I kick and berate myself. Why do I always answer in the affirmative? What if just one time I said, "No"? Would that change anything? Wasn't it at least worth a try? I am so worthless!

When he is all done, he helps me get dressed, and he asks me if I liked it. "Yes", I say, as I always do. There is no need to even tell me anymore that this is our secret. I already know that. And, I will keep this secret just as I always had. I would never betray my daddy.

—⊰+⊱—

I don't know if I was marked goods, or if there was something written on me that said, "Abuse me". But it seemed that for years, I was fair game to anyone who came along, be it other family members or people in my neighborhood. I felt ashamed for not having the courage or the power to make it stop. I didn't even know if anyone out there cared.

I had an uncle who abused me every chance he got. He didn't even care if other people were around or if other children knew what he was doing to me. One Saturday, he came over while my brothers and I were watching cartoons in the living room. My daddy was in his bedroom asleep. My uncle took me into the bathroom, and he did his usual routine with me. He wasn't as kind or gentle as my dad, but either way, I felt like I was just a worthless nothing. But on this particular day, something happened that made me sure that I was just a nothing. When we came out of the bathroom, my daddy was up. My daddy grabbed me roughly by the arm and almost threw me into my bedroom. He then proceeded to have a nice, enjoyable morning with his brother. On that day, I stopped watching cartoons. The sound of a cartoon voice drives me crazy!

There was an incident that happened in my neighborhood with an older teenager that caused a chain-reaction of events that ultimately meant further abuse for me—sexual and mental, though, possibly, it strengthened me spiritually. This older teen was able to physically overpower me. He ripped my clothes off and summoned the other boys in the neighborhood to come look at my naked, struggling body. Most of the boys peered on in amusement. The next day, at school, the girls were whispering about me. A few of the more outspoken girls teasingly and accusingly asked me if I liked it. I inherently knew that in order for me to survive this humiliation, I had to rely on something deep inside of me. I returned to that place often because I knew that no man (not my dad nor uncle), no boy, and no mean girls could ever touch that part of me. That part of me was the real me.

⸻

What has remained consistent through all these years is the distinct impression that there are 2 MEs. There has always been this meek, scared of EVERYTHING me that existed right alongside this all-knowing, confident, can do anything and everything me.

In the early part of my life, I really did not understand the duality. I often vacillated between feeling like some-body was watching me as I lived my life and feeling like I was watching a movie of my life. I sometimes would check around the house looking for a hidden camera.

Back then, the meek, scared of everything me usually took the forefront. But, in times of crisis, the confident me would step in and whisper assurances that everything was going to be okay. Just keep moving forward.

As the years passed, the meek me grew more and more certain that anything the confident me said, could be trusted. I remember not being sure that I could survive the pain from the bad things in my life. Each pain would linger and seem to be inescapable. But that voice, my voice, whispered to me, "You survived before; you can survive this too". Each time I pulled through to the other side, it was like building a muscle that would make it easier to pull through again. Finally, with each affront, I was able to say, this will pass just like it has always passed before. As each year passes, the me who takes the forefront is becoming remarkably similar to the me who watches, confident with a knowing presence.

When I was working on my master's degree at The Ohio State University, I saw a young lady on the "Oprah Winfrey Show" who had no face. She had been tied to a truck and was dragged by two white men simply because she was Black. I was quite taken by this young woman. Her demeanor was unlike what would be expected of someone who had lived through such an unthinkable ordeal. My heart went out to her, but my overwhelming thought was that she was okay. She was okay. How could that be?

I started taking myself through a variety of mental exercises. If I became disfigured for some reason, could I be okay? "No," I said. If I suddenly weren't smart, could I be okay? "No," I said. If I no longer had the ability to be a nice person due to some type of injury to the brain could I be okay? "No," I said.

No? Well, I needed to find a way to turn those "no's" into "yeses". Every day, I repeated those questions to myself. I analyzed why my answers were "No's" and really had to dig deep to figure out what could change those "no's" into "yeses". I recognized that those traits were external to who I was. My appearance and my intelligence and my kindness were not ME. In order to get to the "Yeses", I had to figure out how to value who I really was.

After quite a bit of self-reflection, I was able to get to a yes to the first two questions. But getting to a yes to "If I could no longer be a nice person, could I be okay?" was a much more arduous process. I had a difficult time separating "nice" from who I was. I finally realized that I had to elevate myself from the mundane of the day to day to see a broader picture of the world and my purpose here. If I choose to believe that I am more than the person that I see and that my purpose is bigger and reaches far beyond me, then I can believe that no matter how I show up on this physical world, that my life is purposeful, I have meaning, and there is nothing that can thwart me from leaving the gifts that I have to offer the world.

With this, I realized I had done it. I had finally learned to love myself. As I looked out of the rain-spotted windows of my Ohio apartment, I saw green meadows, beautiful butterflies, and I felt full of bliss. I had experienced bliss in my life once before, but this time it was different. Before, the bliss was totally dependent on my connection with God, something that I saw to be outside of myself. Now, my bliss was from the inside out.

I called my mom, "Mama, I just wanted you to know that if anything happens to me or if I should die tonight, I died truly happy." "Arvat, are you alright? What's wrong?" my mom said with alarm. "No, I called to tell you that finally, I am alright."

I changed my message on my answering machine. It said, "Searching for a love or a friend that will make you happy for always? Search no further. Take a good look into yourself. There you will find true happiness." My friends called and when they would get that message, they would leave me messages that said things like, "That is the corniest message I ever heard." But, I noticed that I received many more phone calls where people were just listening to my answering machine and then hanging up. I think the message rang true for people. I think we instinctively know that we have to turn inward and toward God for all real satisfaction. We just need to be reminded sometimes.

Although I have been aware of the presence of this wiser ME my whole life, I still get amazed when, in times of crisis, the wiser ME steps in and takes over. That ME always knows what to do and executes situations perfectly without missing a beat.

Have you ever heard about situations where people acted courageously and you think to yourself, "Wow, I'm glad I wasn't the person there because I wouldn't have known what to do"? For example, I heard a story about a man, Wesley Autrey, who was waiting on a train at a subway station with his two young daughters when he saw another man who was having a seizure. The man stumbled and fell onto the tracks. Seeing a train approaching, Autrey jumped on the tracks and positioned the man's body in the trench. He then covered the man's body with his own to ensure the man would not move as the train passed over the top of them.

Hearing stories with this level of bravery, quick thinking, and selflessness always leaves me in awe. I wonder what this type of person looks like in his/her day to day life. And, when you hear these types of stories, the person is never impressed with his/herself—"I just did what anybody would do," they all say. If it were me, I would be freaking impressed with myself!

Luckily for me, I rarely find myself in a true crisis anywhere near that magnitude. But there are a few instances that I can recall when I knew that something else stepped in and orchestrated my every move. And, yes, I was freaking impressed!

The sun sat prominently and high, not a cloud in sight. The ocean was the same shade of blue as the sky. We had our beach towels and sunscreen and we talked excitely as we walked onto the beach. Our friends, Floyd and Jolinda, had flown in from the States to visit Harry and me in our home away from home in Barbados.

"Let's rent jet skis," someone had said.

Thinking this was a good idea, "Ok," the rest of us chimed in.

Harry and I hopped on one jet ski while Floyd and Jolinda hopped on another. Soon, we were zooming and the splash from the ocean felt good on our hot skin. I felt that Harry was driving a bit too fast and a bit too aggressively, but I didn't say anything because I was working on not being a nag. Further and further away from shore we went, and the jet ski was often airborne for a second here and there as we crashed into and then hopped over thick, rippling waves.

And, in slow motion, I could see it happening. We were moving too fast to make such a sharp turn. I leaned hard to my left in an effort to provide balance to the jet ski that was destined to flip to the right. But that wasn't enough to overcome the momentum that threw us both off opposite sides of the jet ski.

Thank God for life jackets because neither one of us could swim. But we both maneuvered our way back to the jet-ski.

"Let's flip the jet ski right-side up," Harry said.

We tried but the jet ski was sinking fast. It was no use. I saw Harry's eyes change colors—from a dark brown to a light brown. I instinctively knew that I needed to remain calm. It would kill him to think that I was not ok.

But really, by the looks of things, we were not ok. We were so far away from the shoreline that all I could see was a red dot moving on the beach. I assumed that was someone walking with a pair of red swim trunks. The jet ski was sinking and the tide was pushing us further out and to the west.

"Just hold on. I am going to swim us back to shore," I say to Harry, knowing that what I am saying is not possible.

By now, only the smallest tip of the jet ski was still visible. I assume it was the nose of the jet ski. We both held on to that little tip as I used the other hand to "swim us back to shore."

"Do you think they can see us?" Harry asked.

"I think they are going to realize their jet ski is missing pretty soon and then come looking for us. Besides, Floyd and Jolinda are going to be returning to shore soon and they will send help for us, that is if I haven't gotten us back to shore yet," I say in a matter-of-fact voice.

I kept "swimming us back to shore" as the tide continued to pull us further and further out to sea and far west of the beach where our friends were.

I realized that our "rescue" was taking a long time. It didn't appear that anyone was coming for us after all. But, I, as confidently and as relaxed as ever kept saying, "They will come and get us soon."

Then, out of nowhere, I see the most beautiful sight! A big white sailboat was happening by.

"Are you okay?" a man yells in our direction.

"No," I say.

"You need help?" he asks, already changing his course to come towards us.

"Yes," I say.

"We are okay," I say to Harry.

He nods his head, yes.

The kind strangers took us back to our beach of origin and we were reunited with our friends.

As it turns out, no one was coming to save us. Apparently, the jet ski company only had the two jet skis. The jet ski that Floyd and Jolinda were on stopped working and they were stranded in the middle of the water. The jet ski worker had to swim out to Floyd and Jolinda and tried to get the jet ski started again. No luck. So, they had to be pulled into shore. They had not gotten around to a plan to find us yet. Whew!

We all talked and laughed as we each gave the details of our separate jet ski ordeals. When I got home and had a moment to myself, my entire body began shaking uncontrollably. I started to cry. I could not stop the crying nor the violent trembling of my body. I thought of all of the what ifs. What if a shark that feeds on the reef that surrounds Barbados decided to turn its attention to us? What if any of the big fish around the island had bumped our legs in the water and caused us to panic? What if the nose of the jet ski totally sank and we didn't have anything at all to hold onto? What if those passersby hadn't been passing by to save us? What if, what if, what if?

Obviously, the ME who is afraid of everything and who wouldn't know what to do did not take center stage that day. It was the other ME who knew to be calm and knew what to say and do to ensure that Harry was calm too.

⇥⇤

Over the years, I have come to think of this voice that brings me unscathed through any situation I may encounter, who allows me to go through fire without getting burned, as my Higher Self. I feel an awareness that is watching everything that I do. I feel supported in my decisions. It feels that someone is in my corner, although I perceive that someone to be me, but a wiser, kinder version of myself.

Sometimes, I actually hear a voice, my voice, whispering assurances in my mind. It usually tells me things like, "It's okay," "You are okay," "Keep going" when I feel I am in over my head or when I feel like giving up.

Other times, I feel guided by this presence. I know how to center myself to receive this clear guidance. For example, in my years of working with at-risk adolescents, the youths might run away from home from time to time. I close my eyes and take a couple of deep breaths which immediately takes me to almost a dreamy sort of place. I then say, "If I were _____ (fill in child's name), where would I be?" I then start to drive and I turn my vehicle every time I feel an impulse to turn. Guess what? I always found my child. Sometimes they have been just around the corner at a friend's house. A couple of times, they have been a few counties away. But my guidance system would lead me straight to them. The kids would be so surprised at my presence, they would stop whatever they were doing and just hop in the car with me.

"How did you know I was here?" they would ask.

"Because I know you," I would say with a smile.

When I was an employee, I loved getting my employee evaluation. I looked forward to receiving feedback from my employer or supervisor to get a gauge of what I was doing well and what I needed to focus on next. I liked having goals to work towards and I liked knowing that someone was paying enough attention to me to know what my strengths and needs were.

It wasn't until I became the employer did I realize that everyone did not feel the same way about evaluation day. People were nervous, tense, and fearful about their first evaluations. Some people would enter the office already trembling or with tears in their eyes.

I always wrote meaty, thorough evaluations. I tried to cover as close to every aspect of their performance as I could. I repeatedly received the same feedback from the employees during these evaluations. "How can you know all of this about me?" "It is very accurate." "I didn't know you knew me like this." "Thank you so much." "Can I get a hug?" "I was afraid coming in here, but now I feel really good."

At first, my thinking was, "I work with you every day. Of course, I know you. I pay attention."

But then I realized that I used the exact technique for finding the youths as I used for writing the evaluations. I close my eyes, take a couple of deep breaths, go to that dreamy place, and I put myself into the flow of the person that I am evaluating. From that place, I can easily see and feel the person. I know their strengths, weaknesses, desires, and motivations. And I transfer all of that knowledge to paper.

My Higher Self has also chimed in and guided my steps in times of stress. These are times when the situation calls for quick, on-my-feet thinking. During these times, I do not have to center myself. This guidance just kicks right in. This is a slightly different guidance from when it takes completely over like it did during the jet ski situation. Instead, I feel that I am being given a specific set of instructions and prompted exactly when to carry out each step.

This guidance usually shows up in order to calm other people in crisis down. With the kind of work that I was doing, this was an essential skill to have. Sometimes I would get emergency phone calls because some situation had escalated too far out of control and it was at a point where someone was likely to get hurt.

I would be able to walk right into the middle of the crisis and diffuse the situation and calm down all players. Within moments, people would hand me their chosen weapons and all of the rage and anger would be replaced with remorse and tears.

Was it because I was so smart? Nope. I never really knew what to do. But my Higher Self did. My Higher Self provided me with information such as the expression I needed on my face, where I needed to stand, who to give eye contact to and when, how my voice needed to sound and more. I simply followed the instructions.

I share these stories because I know that everyone has access to this flow of energy that connects us to all that we need.

Stepping into this flow of energy is experienced differently by different people. My personal conceptualization is that at the core of our beings, we are all connected to everyone and to everything. I believe that God is all things at the same time. Therefore, we all are a part of God. Using the human hand to illustrate, I see us each like fingers—separate, similar yet unique, and all connected to the same source. I see us all as having a Higher Self that is intimately aware of this connection at all times and is able to access anything and everything that exists in the field of all that is. Though I rely on that much wiser voice that I experience as my own for guidance, I pray to God whenever I see other people suffering or being mistreated. I pray to God requesting peace and correction in my own life. And, when I am offering love and gratitude, I offer it in the direction of God, knowing that goes out to the entirety of the universe.

However, my mom listens to the voices that she experiences as her Angels. She feels that we each are surrounded by Angels who will respond on our behalf to assist us with any aspect of our lives—all we need to do is ask.

Needless to say, others may rely on their religion or practice of choice and gain access to this flow of energy by way of Jesus, Buddha, Allah, Jehovah, or Krishna to name a few.

From my limited perspective, it doesn't matter how you gain conscious access to the flow of energy that is present and available all the time. What matters is that you become aware of it and begin stepping into it in order to make the world a better place and to make your own life experience more loving, more joyful, and more prosperous.

Possibly due to my incessant talking or maybe due to some other profound reason, when I was a child, my mom regularly made me take breaks. She would say, "Go to your room and learn to be by yourself." Although she would always catch me off-guard and the transition from being around everyone to going to my room alone would be abrupt, I never hesitated to follow her instruction. I knew that I would enjoy the time to myself and that I would come back smarter than when I left the group. I no longer recall what I would do when I was alone but I distinctly remember that I could hear my thoughts. It was as if I would split into two different people—one ME was very similar to the kid who had just left the group and the other ME, my Higher Self.

I believe it was that time in my room by myself that encouraged me to be aware of the duality. During that quiet time, I was developing my own special relationship with my connection to this flow of energy, much in the same way as I would develop any other relationship. Basically, I acknowledged the presence of my Higher Self. I spent quality time and listened to this voice when it talked to me. I trusted its guidance and acted on its instructions. I was appreciative of its presence, its intervention, its support. I sometimes nurtured, but always respected and loved that special part of me.

A relationship like this one is obviously one of the most important relationships I could ever have. So, even though I have often taken it for granted and sometimes I forget to even say, "Good morning," it is worth romancing like no other. When all is going well in my world, I remember to take some time each day just to be quiet. I have learned over the years that I cannot hear my Higher Self speaking to me as clearly when I am stressed and rushed and uptight. It's like I squeeze off the communication channel.

So, for me, taking time out to be still and do nothing is one of the most important things I can do to reclaim my ability to feel and be moved by this flow of energy that is here for me for the asking. The time that I spend here each day probably saves me hours of headaches. It is worth the investment. It makes the flow of my life easier and much more satisfying. So, I unplug from the television, from the phone, from the internet, and the radio. I unplug from the many things that I have to do and from Harry and from my friends.

When I was a business owner, sometimes literally working around the clock, I would make sure all the youths with whom I worked were contently engaged in a specific activity.

Then I would tell them, "I am going to the bathroom for 10 minutes. Do not knock on the door unless someone is at risk of losing a limb." Of course, that didn't stop them from knocking on the door. But they were okay with me not answering it.

Obviously, it is best to have this quiet time when no one is likely to distract me, so I like to do it early in the mornings while most other folks are still sleeping. But sometimes I take it where I can get it—oftentimes, sitting in my car in a parking lot or even right outside of my house.

I know that other people hear that voice of guidance or that feeling that urges them to do certain things, too, even though they may not recognize that they do. I'm sure you hear other people say things like, "Something told me..." or "I don't know how I knew, but I just knew" or "I just acted on instinct" or "I followed my gut". I believe that all of these are instances of people being aware of that something extra that can guide us through this journey that we call life.

From my experience, the more attention you give this energy, the more it will respond to your call. And the more you listen, the more it will talk to you. So, give it a try. Start seeking out this energy that is all around us. Listen for and trust the guidance. As you start to be aware of this relationship, you will automatically feel the gratitude as your life begins to blossom.

It is important to consistently nurture this relationship. I know for me, sometimes it is exactly when I need this help the most that I will allow stress to close off my ability to hear this guidance. When I take a moment to realize that things are harder than they should be, that is when I stop, be still, and be quiet. I refocus my energies and soon, I step back into the magical flow of all things good.

CHAPTER 10
WE ARE ALREADY HERE

To fly as fast as thought, to anywhere
that is, you must begin by knowing
that you have already arrived.

—Richard Bach, *Jonathan Livingston Seagull*

"Imagine," my brother said, "a light covered with a lamp shade that is then covered with a cloth. This can make the light appear pretty dim. But really, the light is shining brightly. That is how all of us are. Our true brilliance is covered by a veil, so we forget that it is there. But all any of us have to do is to pull off the cloth; pull off the shade, and let our light shine."

"And," he said, "this light is not in some of us, it is in all of us. We are the light."

His words about us all being lights rings so true to me. I notice that the brighter I let my own light shine, the easier it is for me to see everyone else's light. The more I let go of stresses and fears and angry thoughts, the more there is nothing to feel stressed or fear or anger about. The more I radiate love out into the world, the more loving the world becomes to me. The more I see myself living a life that I love, the more colorful and fun and robust each day becomes.

To be able to see the light in everyone around me and to be able to garner this wonderful energy from the world, I do the daily practices that I learned to do on those cliffs in Barbados that overlook the pulsating ocean.

For several years after returning home from the island that made my heart sing, I felt that I was unable to return to that meditative bliss. There was no sun rising out of the ocean, no sea salt breeze, no sounds nor smells that calmed the senses. I simply felt unable to vibrate in that frequency of love when I was back home in my concrete surroundings.

Slowly but surely, my light began to seem dim, and the fog settled around the lights that had previously shone so brightly from everyone else. Minor frustrations here and there. Roads blocked where I had once run freely. And, rather than unending bliss, I began living life day by day— putting out the little fires that came along.

But then I remembered: One of my favorite ideas from Deepak Chopra was/is to offer a gift to everyone you meet:

I was fond of taking walks at a particular park because of its peaceful, shady, mile-long loop. Generally, there may only be one or two other people on the loop so it is a perfect place to have time alone in nature. A husband-wife team began frequenting the park while I was there. They walked clockwise around the loop and I walked counter-clockwise. That meant that we passed each other twice on every lap around the loop. For weeks, each time we passed each other, they would be so engrossed in their conversation that they never had even a second to look up to acknowledge my presence.

One day, I decided to offer them a gift, in the way Chopra had suggested. As they approached me, I looked at the husband and I said, only in my mind, "Wow! You have a really great laugh. I bet you are telling your wife an amazing story right now. That is awesome that you have so much to share with her." It was as if I had called his attention out loud because, in that moment, he looked directly at me, smiled broadly, and said, "It's a great day for a walk, isn't it?"

Startled at his immediate response, I began giving gifts to people, only in my mind, in ways big and small. And, I know, beyond a shadow of a doubt, that most people actually do receive them.

—✠ ✠—

And I remembered that God is everywhere all the time. God is in all things. Accepting the God in me makes it easy to accept the God in all else. See, it was easy to see God in the pristine waters and in the vivid arcs of color in the sky, but can you see God infused in the air that we breathe, in the foods that we eat, in the homes that we live, or in that rude guy who lives on your street?

"Argh! My chest is getting tight. I have to fire someone tomorrow. I really don't know what to say to them and I know things are going to get ugly," I whined to my mom at this grown-up responsibility that I was tasked with carrying out.

"Oh, that is easy," she said to me. "Tonight, once you have settled down, send your spirit to his. See yourself offering him pure love. There are no conflicts. Just enjoy being in each other's presence in the presence of love. Tomorrow, he will know that you came to him."

At that time, the idea seemed a little strange to me, but I did not ask any questions. She had been giving me quirky little ideas that my logical, rational mind couldn't fully grasp for as long as I could remember. I had learned over the years that she was usually right, so, by now, I was in the habit of obediently implementing whatever (crazy) ideas she might suggest.

That night, I closed my eyes and took some deep breaths. I then imagined that the best part of me went to the best part of him and I greeted him with love. I then saw us dancing a delightful, elegant, happy dance. There were no words, just this divine dance. When I came out of my trance, I was smiling.

"Mwalimu Larry," I called him to my office the following morning.

"Yes, Mwalimu Arvat. I'm coming. I already know what you want. And I just want you to know that I understand. I would have fired me too. I really love working here but I just couldn't get myself together. I want you to know that I love you; I love all of the walimu and all of the watoto. Y'all haven't seen the last of me. I will still be around. And I want you to make sure that you don't overwork yourself and, please, take some time to eat." With that, he gave me a big hug and began packing his things.

I never said a word. His departure was rather beautiful.

I have consistently used that technique all of the years since that day. If I know I have to go into a situation that has the potential to be explosive or into a situation that may cause me anxiety, I send my spirit to the person's spirit and I dance a loving, happy dance with them. I like to think of it as working things out in advance. These dances have served me well.

Much more recently, in my *A Course in Miracles* group which my brother facilitates, he has been driving home the concept of us all being lights.

"God made us in His image from the same stuff that God is made of. We are not *in* His Kingdom. We *are* His Kingdom," he said. "What we want to do is spend more time remembering who we really are and more time inter-acting with other people as they really are." He goes on to remind us, "We are spirits having a human experience."

His words call attention to the distinctions between *getting v. having* and *becoming v. being*. See, whether I concep-tualize us as God's Kingdom or as integrated into the flow of energy that is always present in all things, how can there be anything lacking? We have access to everything that is present. We just have to know where to look. You don't have to *get* anything. You *have it now*. You don't have to *become* anything. You *are it now*.

Whenever I am using my limited knowledge and come to the conclusion that there is no way to make a thing hap-pen, I strive to remember that, in the whole wide world of possibilities, there has to be at least a million ways that God could get it done. And I know that the perfect method will show up for me exactly when I need it.

This reminds me of a story I once heard: There was a soldier whose enemies were on the verge of overtaking him. He ran as fast as he could to escape. His enemies were quickly gaining on him, so he hid in a cave. While in the cave, he closed his eyes and desperately prayed, "Please, God, save me." When he opened his eyes, he saw a spider making a web across the entrance of the cave. He almost giggled and thought, "I asked to be saved. I wanted a brick wall, but I get a spider web." The soldier heard his enemies approaching and their footsteps slowed when they approached the cave. He continued to pray but was certain this would be the end for him. Then he heard a voice say, "There is no need to search this cave. If he had gone in here, he would have broken the spider web." The enemies moved on and the soldier's life was spared.

In a field where all things are possible, obstacles big and small can be overcome. Important and unimportant dreams can unfold. Life can be a wonderful playground when we realize who we really are and who everyone around us really is, too. We are lights. We only need to remove that shade so that we can shine.

CHAPTER 11
GO AHEAD, DO IT ANYWAY

*I learned that courage was not the absence
of fear, but the triumph over it.*

—*Nelson Mandela*

I n addition to our beliefs, fear is the other thing that keeps
us paralyzed in a life that falls short of what we want and
what we are capable of achieving. Obviously, a good case
can be made for why some fears can be beneficial, but, even
so, allowing the fear to stop our forward movement is the
culprit to be aware of.

Quite honestly, for most of my life, I have been afraid of
everything. And when I say everything, I mean *everything*.
People who know me are often shocked to hear this tidbit
about me.

"You seem fearless. You are always doing stuff that other people just don't do," people often tell me.

When I think about what they are saying, I understand their perspective. I have jumped (or maybe I was pushed) out of an airplane and I have swung from treetops on a high-ropes course in New Zealand. I have patted a spotted leopard and have ridden an elephant through the brush in Botswana. Harry and I packed our bags and moved to a foreign country without knowing another soul there or where we were going to be living. The first time I drove a stick-shift, I was alone in rush-hour traffic in an unfamiliar city after only a five-minute lesson. I learned to ride a bike, how to swim and to kayak all after the age of 40, and I once biked and kayaked clear across the Florida Keys (over 100 miles). Harry and I have explored countries all over the world, usually traveling with no organized groups or other traveling companions. I have sat in a zodiac boat in Antarctica and been so close to the giant humpback whales that I could touch them. I stop and chat with homeless people on the street (which people tell me is dangerous). I have found some of the most amazing, breath-taking views because I always want to see what is around the next bend, "Let's go just a little bit further," I always say. And, in general, I say, "Yes," to challenges and adventures when it would be so much easier, so much safer to say, "No".

I remember my first trip on an airplane. I was 21 years old. I was traveling alone on a six-hour flight to Las Vegas and I was terrified! I committed every detail of my flight itinerary to memory because, with so many planes to choose from, I wanted to make sure I got on the right one. My heart raced—the sound of the door of the plane closing and the rumble of the engine and the whirl of the propellers, the chimes and the voices of the flight attendants as they checked and cross-checked for all systems go in the cabin, and the backward momentum as the plane pushed from the gate. I grabbed the armrests of my seat and clenched my teeth as tightly as I could as the plane accelerated down the runway. My back was forced to my seat as the plane went airborne. My ears began popping and my mouth began watering. I took deep breaths and I prayed to prevent myself from crying when everyone around me looked as cool as cucumbers. I remained on high alert, even after the plane balanced itself and we were in cruise mode.

Soon enough, the plane began to bounce and shake and I was certain this was the end. I grabbed the armrests again and my eyes were wide like golf balls. The people around me didn't seem to notice that we are about to plummet to our deaths. They continued to read or to sleep or to chat with their neighbor like nothing was even happening. A tear fell from each of my eyes, but I took my cue from the folks around me and I tried to keep my composure. The plane stabilized but I never relaxed. Each time my heart rate began to de-escalate, the entire scenario was repeated—bounce, shake, terror!

And, while I was glad when I heard that we were making our final approach and would be landing in Las Vegas soon, if I had been less well, I am sure that I would have had a heart attack. I felt the plane jerk as the compartments opened to expose the landing gear, and the plane skipped and jumped when the wheels of the plane made first contact with the ground. And, I wasn't sure that the pilot was going to be able to slow that craft down in time to keep us from barreling clear through the bricks and glass of the airport! But he did. And I survived to tell the story.

And I have been flying ever since. Now, I am that passenger who looks un-phased by the bouncing and shaking that occurs when the plane goes through an air pocket or through a rough patch of clouds. However, I still say two little prayers with each rumble—one asking for safety and one of gratitude for making it to the other side of each rumble.

Being afraid to fly the first time is probably a very common fear. But I can be afraid at the thought of making simple phone calls like calling to set up a doctor's appointment or to get a taxi or to seek information. I can be afraid to tell the waiter that my order is wrong or to ask someone for directions or to talk to people at parties. I can even be afraid that I am going to be too afraid to do whatever the next thing is.

My typical way of handling fear has been to be courageous. In other words, I am afraid as heck, I say some prayers, hold my breath, and then run in as fast as I can. Sometimes I spend time thinking, "What is the worst thing that can happen?" and "If that happened, can I find a way to still be okay?" That is why I love these lyrics from a song by Pink:

Where there is desire, there is gonna be a flame
Where there is a flame, someone's bound to get burned
But just because it burns, doesn't mean you're gonna die
You gotta get up and try, and try, and try.

I have spent enough time dipping into the hard knocks of life to know that I can bounce back from anything. So, what's the harm in trying?

But mostly, I follow the guidance of my Higher Self. If I feel that push or hear that little voice saying, "It's going to be okay", then I move forward, expecting the best.

CHAPTER 12

BEING FEARLESS

There is nothing to fear but fear itself.

—*Franklin D. Roosevelt*

I am moving towards a new way of handling fear. Rather than being courageous, I have my sights on becoming fearless. If I banish my fears, then I have no reason to be brave. If being fearful can cause me to limit what is possible for me, then being fearless has the potential to expand my possibilities.

I know what you are thinking. Aren't many of our fears healthy and maybe even necessary? Aren't many of our fears automatic—that fight or flight response? Isn't it the fear of getting burned that keeps you from putting your hand in the fire (both literally and figuratively)? Isn't it the fear of causing injury to self and others that causes you to take caution while driving? Isn't it the fear of not being able to pay your bills that keeps you going into that job that you hate? Isn't it the fear of falling that causes you to not walk too closely to the edge? Isn't it the fear of being abused that causes you to hold your tongue when that cop pulls you over for no apparent reason? Isn't it the fear of being attacked that keeps you from walking down dark streets?

And, I do realize that many of our fear responses are automatic. If someone or something is chasing you, you run. If you see a tree about to fall, you get out of the way. If something is barreling towards you, you duck or cover your face.

Being afraid of everything, as I have lived my life being, I certainly feel that a solid case can be made for the need/desirability for healthy fears. And, I also believe that some fears are pre-programmed into us without our conscious consent.

However, I am making a conscious effort to make all my fears disappear. I did not say that I am making an effort to make foolish choices. See, I am not walking around in life being fearful of putting my hand in the fire. I already know from experience that putting my hand in the fire is not a good idea, so I choose to not do that. (Well, that might not be a good example because I did put my bare feet on that blazing hot bed of coals...) But what I am trying to say is that I don't choose to drive carefully or to hold my tongue when speaking to folks because I am afraid of the consequences. I have absolutely no desire to drive recklessly or to be rude to someone just because they are being rude to me. And, I do not think the decision to be a cautious driver or to always treat others with respect are choices that will limit my possibilities.

What I am putting my attention on is being actively engaged in the process of offering pure love to every situation that I fear. For example, I am fearful of talking to people at parties or any function where people do small talk. I feel awkward in those settings and I usually try to make my exit from such situations as quickly as possible. Of course, sometimes I am stuck there. Being a quiet person actually works out quite well when I am with people who have a lot to say. I get to listen and encourage them to continue speaking. But when the conversation turns to me and folks want to know what I think, I never know what to say. My brain freezes. I feel that I couldn't string two words together in a logical order if I tried.

I assume this is a left-over auto-response from yesteryear when I was the ugly, stinky, buck-toothed, too fat-therefore-I-made-men-want-to-touch-me girl who no one liked or wanted to be around. My instinct back then was to hide or to take up as little space as possible so that I wouldn't be seen (or touched). My anxiety would sky-rocket at the thought of having to be around people who might judge, reject, or touch me. So, the best I could do at social functions was to sit in a corner and smile.

The identity that I have carried for most of my life is that of a loner, usually only speaking in response to being spoken to, and preferring to distance myself from most people. I did have a razor-sharp tongue that I could use to slice you if you mess with me, but for as long as I can remember, everyone always referred to me as the sweet, quiet girl. That identity has been my comfort zone.

However, recently I have come to view this identity as a rather self-centered one. Self-centered because I get to be the voyeur who knows everyone, yet no one knows me. People have trusted me with their stories but I don't share any stories back. Self-centered because I am spending my time planning my exit strategy instead of being fully present in the moment. I am thinking about how I can make the situation *less* uncomfortable for me which limits my ability to make the situation *more* comfortable for the people with whom I am engaged.

My solution to remedy this fear and to change this identity—love. See, I am not expecting that all of a sudden I will become a masterful communicator, nor am I sure that I want to be. But when I remember to offer pure love to the situation, it changes everything. Before walking into the event, I center myself and I see myself radiating love through my very pores to all that I meet. Rather than feel anxiety, I feel joy. I greet people at the heart-level instead of allowing my eyes to guide my response. I hear their stories differently. I am more engaged. I put them at ease, and I believe they can feel the love that I am pouring out to them. We both are better because of this interaction.

I am learning to repeat this scenario for situations big and small—rude people, snooty people, racist people, careless people, all people. I am learning to look past whatever face they are presenting and, instead, seeing the divinity in them. It is there that I make a loving connection. Love transforms people and situations right before my very eyes.

But can love banish other kinds of fears too? Absolutely! After having not been in the water to swim in several years, I decided to hop back into the pool. For some reason, as soon as I would start swimming, I would start to feel panicked. The panicky feeling didn't really make sense to me because at the pool's deepest end, the water was only 4 1/2 feet deep. I could easily stand up at any time. The panicky feeling was so disturbing to me that it made me dread going to the pool.

But, then, something triggered a memory for me. I used to mop the floors of the school that I co-founded every evening after the students had departed for home. Like I did in my entire life back then, I always rushed, and I mopped the floor with great vigor. One day, a community volunteer walked in while I was mopping. She immediately took the mop away from me.

"You need to mop the floor like this," she said, gliding the mop across the floor as if she was doing a seductive slow dance. "You see, you have to mop the floor with love. Everything you do in this school needs to be done with love because the children will feel it."

Truthfully, I blew her off. I was just happy that she was now mopping the floor and I was free to begin my next task. But her words stuck with me in the back of my mind.

Using the idea that woman planted in my mind all those years ago, I decided to swim with love. I decided to offer the water love and I envisioned myself moving lovingly through that love-infused water. This new imagery removed the dread that I had begun to associate with getting in the water. And each time I felt a twinge of panic, I would immediately shift my thoughts to that lovely, loving scene of being at one with the water and the panic would fade.

What about the fear of bumble bees?

"Why are you running? That bee is not going to sting you," my friend tells me.

"How do you know?" I ask.

"Have you ever been stung by a bee before?" he asks.

"No, because I always run away from them," I say.

I know—whether or not I get stung by a bumble bee is probably not going to have any long-term effect on my life, but I am practicing replacing fear with love in all aspects of my life. So, now instead of running away from bees, I stand my ground and I send them gratitude for all of the wonderful things they do to help keep our ecology healthy. Plus, I thank them for that delicious honey.

I do the same with dogs. Unlike most Americans, I am not a dog lover. I have been bitten twice by dogs—once as a child and again some 30 years later. Normally, my heart-rate rises and I catch my breath at the sight of an unleashed dog. Now, at the sight of these dogs whose owners say, "He's friendly. He won't bite. He just wants some attention," I start talking to them in my mind. "Hey, cutie. How are you? Aren't you just the sweetest?" I say to them the same way I would talk to a precious, little baby.

I would like to think that I could offer out this love to everybody and everything instead of responding in a fear that causes me to contract or reduce the expression of the best part of me. Now, I can't promise you how I would react if I come face to face with a bear. Like I said, I am learning.

I would imagine that replacing any kind of fear with love can help transform the situation. Whenever you fear you might be judged because maybe you think you are not smart enough or not educated enough or not pretty enough or not witty enough or not thin enough or anything not enough, take your focus off of you and send out your most loving energy to the people or situation. To be clear, I am not suggesting going around hugging on folks and telling them you love them. I mean, in your mind, see yourself dancing a beautiful dance or appreciating their existence on this earth or just beaming your loving energy onto them. We all are attracted to this energy and we unconsciously know when we have stepped into this energy field.

I do have a story where fear truly got the best of me and changed the course of my life. I am making no judgments on the decisions I made at the time and I honestly don't know if I would handle the situation any differently if it happened to me today. But it gives me something to think about.

As I mentioned, living in Barbados was the best time of my life. I grew and changed in ways unimaginable to me. I fell so completely in love with myself, with life, and with everything in the universe. I felt free!

During one of my solo expeditions of the island, I happened upon a most charming nook. It was perched on a cliff that overlooked the calm, Caribbean Sea-influenced waters of Barbados. Due to its secluded location, it was always tranquil, unknown of even by many of the locals. It quickly became one of my favorite spots and I often visited it twice a day. Here, I see the bobbing heads of the giant sea turtles as they come up for air at irregular intervals. From this vantage point, I occasionally see stingrays propel themselves out of the water and into the air. I once saw a humpback whale vacation here for about 3 days. I was filled with glee each time I saw the plume of mist erupt from its blow hole. And I was overwhelmed when it, too, propelled itself from the water, into the air making a huge splash in the otherwise calm ocean.

I took in and marveled at every detail of this nook. There was much to see in the ocean, but I also began to notice the normally mundane aspects of the land. I noticed that right around sunset, the trees would become filled with birds as they returned home in time for their evening curfew. The chirps from the birds would quickly drop from about a million chirps per minute to 1000 chirps per minute to 5 chirps per minute to absolute silence as they quieted themselves for their nightly slumber.

On this cliff was a withering walnut tree that I decided to send healing energy. Every day, I would count the number of walnuts on it and I was amazed how my attention to this tree seemed to bring it back to life. I even watched ants and was fascinated by their daily routines and supreme organization.

One day, a local man found his way into my little sanctuary.

"Morning," he said.

"Good morning," I replied cheerfully.

"Did you go to Crop Over?" he asked, having noticed my American accent.

"No, I didn't go this year," I said. "But I know it was a lot of fun!"

"Yes," he said as he sat down close to me like we were good friends.

We sat in silence for a while and I returned my gaze to all of the beauty around me. He began to smoke a cigarette and the breeze carried the smoke directly into my nostrils.

"That smoke is blowing directly in my face," I told him.

"Oh, I am so sorry," he said as he got up and moved to the other side of me, still so close to me that it seemed we were on a date.

After a few more moments of silence, I got up and moved to stand in a different location where I continued to admire the view, but now my back was to him.

"Oh, my!" I exclaimed as I turned to leave this location. I was startled because he was now standing directly behind me.

"Oh no, no," he said in an attempt to calm me down. "I just wanted to be close to you."

As I was leaving my special nook, I noticed that he had driven a rental car to this location and I took note of the license plate. After my 10-minute walk back to my home, I told Harry about this strange encounter. Alarmed, he had me take him immediately back to the nook, but the man was gone. Harry admonished me for not realizing sooner that I should have gotten away from this man. I was a little surprised at Harry's reaction because I had not registered fear. I had only registered this as strange behavior. But then I began to wonder, "Had I really been in danger and not even realized it?" My gut usually tells me when it is time to get the heck out of dodge. But it had not told me that.

The very next morning, his arrival at my nook shattered my peace and I immediately left to head for home. As I was walking, I saw him drive past me. Then I saw him drive past me again and yet again. I realized that he was following me. My instincts took over and I knew exactly what to do in order to outmaneuver him. Now I realized that I had been in danger.

For the next few mornings, Harry went with me on all of my excursions, and we did not see him. The first morning that I went back out on my own, he was back. And he was following me. Again, I was able to shake him off of my trail. I told one of my Bajan friends about these encounters. After describing the man, my friend said, "Be careful. He just got out of the insane asylum. He follows women to their homes and then breaks in and rapes them when they are at home alone."

Now, I was petrified. For the next couple of months, I never left the house without Harry and I was always on high alert. I continued to do my morning routine which included a run before sunrise. Since Harry was not a runner, I would run a couple of blocks up ahead of him and then run back to him to close the gap as he walked. Since the two encounters I had had with this man (who we began referring to as "The Stalker") was during daylight hours and almost a mile away from my house, I felt fairly safe running a bit ahead of Harry.

Then, one morning, I was doing hill repeats on a hill right in front of my home. I ran up the hill and down the hill and up the hill and down the hill as Harry sat at the bottom of the hill waiting patiently to move on. But from where Harry was sitting, he could not see the top of the hill.

After about my fourth time up the hill, I see that rental car! It was The Stalker! Somehow, I was able to see the look on his face. He was smiling. I took off down the hill as fast as my legs would carry me as I screamed Harry's name over and over. The Stalker followed me closely in his car angling his car towards me as if to try to block my forward movement.

Finally, Harry was in eyesight and he immediately took in the urgency of this situation. He picked up a big cinder brick and was poised to use it as a weapon. The Stalker put his car in reverse and sped backward up the hill. At daylight, we went to the police.

The story is long and involved, but let's suffice it to say that everything changed for me. He continued to stalk me for months and I was in a perpetual state of terror. All of the freedom and joy that I had experienced in my tiny paradise was gone. It was time for me to pack my bags and to return home to the States.

I have thought about The Stalker a lot over the years. I have wondered what energy I was sending out that caused me to lose my coveted home on the southern tip of a perfect island. Why had I drawn this man to me? What was I to learn from all of this?

I have considered many possibilities as to why he and I had been intertwined in this cat and mouse interaction. Lately, I have been considering the possibility that it all had to do with love. On the one hand, I think about how it was so easy for me to be in the flow of love and loving everything around me when everywhere I looked, I only saw beauty. But could I emit such love when the outer shell wasn't beautiful? Although, in the midst of the experience, there were moments in time when I sent love out to The Stalker, I usually was afraid and had angry thoughts towards him.

On the other hand, I think about our first encounter. I was not afraid. I experienced his behavior as strange, yet peaceful. If he wanted to harm me, that would have been the perfect place to do so and there had been ample time. Perhaps the love that I was emitting had been enough to protect me from him. Or maybe my loving thoughts over-rode his thinking. Perhaps he really did just want to sit there, close to me, and drink in the pocket of serenity that I had created on that magnificent cliff.

Don't get me wrong, I do think that the smart thing to do that day was to leave the situation. And knowing all of the things that I eventually found out about him, it was best to arrange my days to avoid seeing him as much as possible. But, instead of constantly thinking about this man, night and day, with fear and terror, perhaps I could have replaced my fear thoughts with love thoughts. Perhaps I could have practiced dancing that loving dance with him in my mind—spirit to spirit. Perhaps we could have worked everything out there, in that place beyond our eyes.

CHAPTER 13
MY RECIPE

Cupcakes are muffins that believed in miracles.

I do not know why God chose to spare my life all those years ago. Nor do I know what the purpose of my youthful struggle has been. But I am glad for each. Back then, I never thought I would see the day when I love living. But now I have decided that I shall live to be 123 years old. That means I have more living to do than I have already done. I am excited about the prospects. I do not know when or if the purpose of my struggles will be revealed to me, maybe tomorrow or maybe one day when I am 123. But, I like the person that I have become as a result. I like that I am able to tell young people who ache to just hold on because the best of their lives are still before them. I like that I am able to move confidently through storms and that I know how to come through the fire without getting burned. I like that

I smile on most days of my life and that I can always find things to laugh about. I like knowing that a bad patch is just one of those things that will pass and will hardly leave a blemish on the fabric of my life. I like that I am able to look into the eyes of anyone and see that I already know them. Of course, I do. They are a part of me. My intention is to be their mirror—to reflect back to them, not just the person who they pretend to be, but the person who they really are. If you see love when you look at me, now you know why—I am a reflection of you.

I share these stories of my life with you not because I think they are a blueprint for life, but because they are a blueprint of *my* life. There have been times in my life when I wished that someone would tell me something, anything to help me make it through, like when I had no idea of how to go about loving myself or when I didn't feel that I had the strength to continue working with the youths who I loved so much.

As I examine my life from the distance that time provides, I can clearly see that I had a charmed life though it may not have felt like it at the time. This shy, poor, scared of everything, suicidal, physically, sexually, emotionally abused little girl with the alcoholic father is truly okay today. Heck, I am fantastic! And I'm intending to get better with each day that passes.

It is my hope that some of the things in this book resonate with you. Maybe you will use something that I have said and bend it in such a way that it fits your life too. Maybe an idea in these pages will spark an even better idea for you. The point of this book is that we don't have to settle for what life has presented to us; we get to choose the life that we want. By virtue of being a Black female in America, someone or something has already chosen some of your circumstances and has possibly limited some of your aspirations. But the truth is that we get to say, "I am capable of choosing for myself, thank you very much." We don't have to play the game that is already on the table. We can decide on the game that we want to play.

One thing that I have learned from visiting many countries is that people from all over the globe are watching us. When Black people in America have successes, people from countries around the world cheer. Some cheer because they recognize our hardships and they are happy when they see good things happening for us. But others cheer because they know that if we "broke through", it is just a matter of time before they come through too. So, they are looking to us to help elevate the status of people everywhere. Black woman, when you speak your unique voice into the universe, not only will the universe respond to you, but it will sing a sweet melody that ripples through you and far, far beyond.

Though our rich history far exceeds these shores, our collective psyche is parked on our past and current day struggles. We suffer from a wound that cut deeply into every fiber of our being. As with any wound, we need time to heal. With a physical wound, we go through a process of removing our bandages, cleansing the wound, soothing the pain and re-bandaging it. Before the healing is fully completed, we remove the bandages for good. We expose our wounds to the light and allow the scabs to fall off. Eventually, the scars will disappear.

Our great women, from all walks of life, have helped to remove the bandages, cleanse, soothe, and re-bandage our wound by offering their distinctive passions to the world. And each cycle of cleansing and bandaging has brought us closer to healing. Our healing may not be complete today, but much of the work has already been done for us. Let us remove the bandage this final time by letting our dreams unfold. Let us see the light and be the light that shines that makes the scabs fall off. Our entire world seems to be at a tipping point, and it needs you, Black woman, to whisper your desires and passions into the far reaches of the universe. Your voice matters. Your happiness matters. Your love matters.

I have long suffered from the Smart People Syndrome. I thought I knew everything. I am only kidding when I say that, but the truth is that because I could logically figure out a way to do most things, I often failed to utilize the energy that surrounds me every day—that field where everything is possible. I have relied on intellect, my ability to endure, and brute force to take steps forward in life. Those things do work to a certain degree, but that is the hard way and sometimes joyless way of doing things. I have finally learned the recipe that works for me that allows me to experience my greatest dreams and all of the colors of the rainbow.

The four main ingredients in my recipe are:

- Being aware that I am more than what meets the eye. I am a part of all that is. I am connected to everything that has been and that ever will be. I have direct access to this flow of energy.
- Understanding the power of my thoughts. I know that I have to think it in order to create it. So, I allow myself time to think. I think about what I want in life and I think about how I can use my distinct passions to help other people to live lives that they love. I realize that I have to allow my thoughts to become a part of me. So, if I want to be a better swimmer, I read about people who swim well; watch videos of swimmers, and envision my body moving the way great swimmers' move their bodies.
- Understanding the power of my imagination. I use my imagination to envision anything that I want. If I want something, I use my imagination to see and feel that thing. I pull that thing closer and closer to me the more that I spend time giving it my attention and love. I think about how I would feel if I were experiencing that thing and then I practice feeling that thing all day long. So, if I want to be a certain weight, I imagine how I would feel, what I would think, how I would dress, how I would eat, etc. and then I attempt to feel that feeling all day long. I believe that any amount of time that you spend thinking about and imagining the things that you want is way better than

not thinking about it at all. But the more that you can touch, taste and feel it, the sooner it is going to show up. Another thing about the beauty of imagination is that it is MY imagination. I am free to envision anything that I want. If I don't like the way something is, I just create a vision of something that suits me better—because if I believe it to be true, then it is true for me even if it is not true for you. In a world of infinite possibilities, I believe both *this* and *that* can be true.

- Recognizing the transformative power of love. Even when people are not behaving in loving ways, I am becoming more able to see them as the true light that they are and to see them as a loving extension of myself. The more able I am to recognize our sameness and to flow love to them, the easier situations resolve themselves. So, I practice offering everyone and everything, including myself, the gift of love.

Feel free to use my recipe, if you'd like. You may find that to make it your own, you might add a little more sugar or a little less spice. You may decide you want nuts or you may get rid of the flour altogether. The point is that we already have exactly what we need to live a life that we want. We have to know where to look. Just like I have my stories of the trials and errors I have experienced on my way to finding myself in a life that I love, I know that you have your stories too. Look at your stories and see how you made it through each time. What magical little things showed up to pull you through?

You have access to that magic, not just in times of need but at all times. Choose for yourself what your new identity will be and live in that identity. Choose an identity of love and joy and freedom and abundance and health and success and of one who makes her dreams come true.

Black woman, allow the universe to pulsate to the beat of your heart and the rush of your desires. This is the gift that *you* were singularly made to offer to the world to help the world express itself as God's perfect masterpiece.

ACKNOWLEDGMENTS

I n this moment, I am feeling so thankful that it is hard for me to focus my energy on just a few individuals to acknowledge. In my mind, I am seeing images of so many ancestors and contemporaries, known and unknown, who have uniquely shined their lights in ways that have made my journey possible. It feels almost disrespectful to name only a few. But I am thankful for all of the people who, through example, showed me that it is okay to be smart, be different, have dreams; that it is possible to love life, be beautiful, be adventurous; that we can challenge the status quo, be successful, and be winners. Thank you, Harriet Tubman, Michelle Obama, Oprah, Cicely Tyson, Diana Ross, Mae Jemison, George Washington Carver, Nelson Mandela, Barak Obama, Douglas L. Wilder, Malidoma Patrice Some'...

Since I was a pre-teen, self-help and spiritual books helped to guide me through my rocky path and gave me a reason to hold on a bit longer. I am forever grateful to the people who took the time to write these informational and inspirational messages—again, way too many to name but include Les Brown, Iyanla Vanzant, Tony Robbins, Deepak Chopra, Wayne Dyer, and Gary Zukav.

A little closer to home is that group of people who cheer for me no matter what I do. Your unending support is priceless to me and makes me feel like I can do anything! This includes my family by choice: CD, Richard, Alfonso, Mickey, Keisha, Greg, Clarence B., Jeanette, Flamonda, Zari, Jan, Bernard and Kim, Anthony, Darryl, Nelson, Anne, Tonya, Hollee, Juanita, Tammy, Thomas, Mark, Karen, Khilia, Joe, David and Gee, Jamal, Denise, Vincent, Monica, Michelle, Nate, Korantema and Abena, Auntie Marie, Mama Marie, Mama Mary, Mama Virginia, Chris, Francia, Thadey, Mike and Aster (and Destana, Selam, and Zhema), the members of the SEAL Team PT, and all of the old members of River City Runners of Color. And, my, "sorry, but you are stuck with me" family: Marcus, Raponyer, Jaconyer, William, Rivanna, Uncle Noah, Uncle Butch and Aunt Sarah, Harry's mom (lol—Barbara), Rodney, Kylan, Terron, Ayanna, Charita, Stacy and Bridgette, Terrance and Chandra, Boo and Sharon (and their awesome children), Wanda, Aunt Mildred, Helen and Bowman, and Glo Mae.

As for writing *this* book, a hearty THANK YOU goes out to Tracy McGuire who could never guess how much her simple yet consistent question of, "Arvat, when are you going to write your next book?" inspired me to continue to write over the years. Gary, Maurice, Lloyd, Derrick, and Debbie, thank you for listening to or reading early chapters of the book and giving feedback that inspired me to move forward with my writing. The fact that I trusted you with my work so early in the game, speaks volumes. Also, my editor, Victoria West, couldn't have been more supportive. For that, I am thankful.

A special thank you to my loudest, proudest cheerleaders who applauded me at each tiny milestone, who buoyed me through my doubts, and who never had a doubt in me. Thank you for your insights, the magnificent roles you play in my life, for showering me with unending love, for being on TEAM ARVAT: Mama, Marie, Nin Aseeya, Sandy, Vinceretta, Scott and Angela, and Dianna.

And, finally, what can I say to the amazing man with whom I am blessed to share my life? Being a witness to the love that you pour out so easily to the world keeps me in a constant state of awe. Your, seemingly, effortless ability to make your (and my) dreams come true is a marvel. To be able to hear your hearty laugh is what makes me excited about each new day. Your heart-song flows into my heart which then overflows into many rivers beyond. Harry, thank you.

BOOK CLUB DISCUSSION QUESTIONS

1. Arvat opens the book describing her beautiful drive to her newly built dream home, Uhuru Bluff, named after Uhuru Peak at the top of Mount Kilimanjaro in Tanzania ("uhuru" means "freedom" in Swahili). Her home is located moments away from an abandoned Confederate Army site, as well as cotton fields once worked by enslaved men and women. Why did she become angry on her drive? Do you think her anger was justified? On that day in January, she had a perspective shift. What was the shift and how do you think she arrived at this new perspective?

2. Arvat compares the dreams of Harriet Tubman, Martin Luther King, Jr., and Nelson Mandela to our own dreams. Do you think this is a fair comparison? Why or why not?

3. What do you think of the ombre' dress idea—the idea that we are all connected, that our energy fields

radiate out to the entire world, that what we do matters?

4. Throughout the book, Arvat points out her habitual instinct to figure things out for herself and to try to *make* things happen. However, she realizes that when she relies on that field of energy to which we all have access, life is much easier and unfolds almost magically. What are examples in your own life when you have let go of the reins and relied on your own faith? What miracles have happened in your life? What "impossible" situations have you overcome? She also says that she does all that she can do—studies, trains, works—and then asks for help. Do you think this is a necessary step? Why or why not?

5. What beliefs do you have surrounding struggle? Do you feel that life is a struggle? That things are supposed to be hard? That something is only worthwhile if you had to fight for it? Do you ever feel guilty for your own successes? Envious of others' successes? How might your personal beliefs about struggle and success affect the way you experience life?

6. In Chapter 5, Arvat wrote: "What I noticed all those years ago is that things *are not* always what you think they are. What I notice today is that things *are* always what you think they are." What does this mean to you? How have you seen this play out in your own life or the lives of people you know?

7. Arvat talks about how our thoughts and beliefs determine our behaviors. She mentioned three methods that she has used when she wanted to change old behaviors or begin new behaviors. What methods

do you use to change old or create new behaviors? What methods seem to work the best for you?

8. Most of us are familiar with the idea of visualizing what you want and pulling that thing toward you by spending time with it in your mind. But some of the things we want never seem to show up. In Chapter 8, Arvat briefly mentions getting clear on her intentions. She had been praying that God relieve her of some of her burdens. But after examining her true intentions, she realized that she hadn't really wanted to serve *less* people; she wanted to be able to serve *more*. By being clear on her intentions, she was able to pray a new prayer and ask to feel connected to God's unending flow of love. This new prayer changed her life. Is there an area in your life where you can examine your true intentions to see if they line up with what you are praying/asking/hoping for?

9. Arvat mentions another part of herself that she calls her Higher Self which guides her if she takes the time to listen to it. Have you ever received this kind of guidance? How does this guidance communicate with you? What do you do or what can you do to hear this guidance more clearly?

10. Arvat alludes to the Divinity in us all when she speaks of us as all being lights. Do you think it is possible for us to access that part of ourselves that is pure love and free of judgments and "dance" or connect with someone else's field of pure love?

11. What is the difference between being courageous and fearless? Is it possible, or even desirable, to be fearless?

12. Arvat says we are free to choose for ourselves our identities, our dreams, and the gifts that we will offer the world. What are your dreams? What are your desires? What gifts do you choose to pulsate out into the world?

ABOUT THE AUTHOR

Arvat McClaine, Ph.D., married to the boy next door (Harry Watkins) for 23 years, is a perpetual student of life with a personal motto of "Better and better every day." Arvat enjoys laughing, exploring in nature, exercising, traveling, having quiet time, reading, thinking, dreaming and inspiring others to make their dreams come true.

48071309R00098

Made in the USA
Middletown, DE
10 September 2017